Heal Not Lightly

Heal Not Lightly

Harry Smith

New Wine Ministries

New Wine Ministries
PO Box 17
Chichester
West Sussex
United Kingdom
PO19 2AW

ISBN 1–903725–73–9

Cover concept by David Henderson
Chapter heading graphics by Camilla Håkansonn
Typeset by CRB Associates, Reepham, Norfolk
Printed in Malta

Dedication

I dedicate this book to the Rev. Cecil and Myrtle Kerr, thanking them for their sacrificial giving of themselves not only in the setting up and overseeing of the ministry of the Christian Renewal Centre in Rostrevor from 1974 to 2001, but also for their commitment to Christ's ministry of reconciliation in Ireland. I also want to thank my wife Dorothy, family, community members of the Centre and friends of the ministry here for all their loving support, encouragement and prayers over the past eleven years as the contents of this book have developed.

Contents

Foreword

There is something sinister to our modern minds about the idea of a blood covenant. Yet the idea of a covenant, according to many dictionaries, stems from the covenant God made with His people, the children of Israel. In Scripture, covenants are variously described. In Genesis 9:9 it is with and through Noah. In Genesis 15:18 it is with and through Abraham. In Exodus 19:15 it is with and through His people. And so it goes on throughout the Old Testament through priests, kings and prophets, culminating in the prophesied New Covenant, which was implemented through the sacrifice of Christ on the cross. He therefore became the mediator of this New Covenant (Hebrews 9:15), through which our consciences, hearts, minds and spirits are cleansed. There is finality about this covenant too – it is once, for all. There remains no further need for sacrifice. He made one sacrifice for sins, forever.

This is standard doctrine for believers in Christ. This is what we have understood, believed in and spiritually embraced. It is foundational to our faith. So to have discovered that the majority of the Protestant spiritual and political forebears in Northern Ireland made a fresh covenant in 1912 – some signing it in blood, with countless others willing to lay down their lives for it – raises for many, serious questions about its necessity, its biblical warranty and its basis.

Many pagan worshippers make covenants and sacrifices in blood before their pagan deities – sometimes by human or animal sacrifice. This practice still continues in various forms in many parts of the world, where the worship of a god or goddess is so entangled with national identity that young men and women can make a vow of allegiance to their god or nation, even to the ultimate cost – the sacrifice of their own lives – and even signing it in their own blood. It may not be right, but it can occur if there is no other spiritual light.

But why have Christian leaders been led to do something similar? And what spiritual effect has this had? And can something be done about this retrospectively? And will it make a difference?

Harry Smith in this book seeks answers to these questions, believing, as he does, that the spiritual consequences of the signing of the Ulster Covenant nearly a century ago have not adequately been understood before. He sees the devastating consequences in terms of generations of young men of Ulster whose lives have been laid down, without apparently achieving anything more than endless violence, bloodshed, hatred and fear. He believes that there is need for that Covenant – at various levels – to be renounced in order to break this cycle. He sees that the fruit can only be affected by dealing with the root.

I warmly welcome this contribution, written by a man I have known for more than eighteen years. Like many other Northern Irishmen I have met, who had moved out of this cycle of violence in order to seek to serve God in a more congenial setting elsewhere in the world, Harry used to despair of seeing any lasting change. But unlike many of these, he has followed God's call to move back into the hard place in order to seek to work out, through prayer and reconciliation, another way. He has worked and prayed with both Catholics and Protestants, and carries a spiritual prayer burden for the whole of the island of Ireland. He has also carried this burden about the Ulster Covenant for many years. I have been one of those who have encouraged him to pursue his research and his mission and to engage with church and political leaders on the issues. I have also been with him through the tears and spiritual agony that is part of his journey. Like many in the intercession and reconciliation movement, he believes that our first appeal has to be to God, then to the church. Eventually (or maybe sooner) the appeal will be to politicians also.

I too want to see change in Ireland. Having been scores of times to pray and weep over the pain of Ireland, and minister in the spirit of reconciliation, my prayer is that God will use this to spark a significant movement for change. We are tripartite beings, made up of body, mind and spirit, worshipping a Triune God – Father Son and Holy Spirit. In this book Harry seeks to appeal to all three parts of our being. It is my prayer that readers will engage with this in the same way.

As I was saying, there is something sinister about a blood covenant – that is, one either signed in blood or made with the intent of laying down one's life for something.

Brian Mills
Sussex, England,
May, 2006

Brian Mills, former prayer secretary for The Evangelical Alliance (UK), currently an Associate of the International Reconciliation Coalition, and leader of the Interprayer International Partnership.

Introduction

At last! I have put pen to paper – or is it fingers to keyboard? After much prayerful consideration, struggling, encouragement and cajoling, I have decided to write about a journey I have made over the last eleven years, a journey on my own and with other people, in prayer, reading and research, one which I believe has far reaching consequences for the Ireland of tomorrow.

It was not self-initiated but rather, I believe, started with God. To be precise, it all started with a dream (or was it a vision?). It was so clear – both visually and audibly – that it is as clear today as it was when I first experienced it. In fact, it could be said that nearly everything I share with you in this book stands or falls on the question, 'Was it of God?'

I had a deep encounter with God in the early 1970s, as the Charismatic Renewal Movement swept through Ireland. Many people during the ensuing years had spoken of God speaking to them through prophecies, visions, dreams or pictures. 'The word of the LORD came to ... ' is mentioned ninety-eight times in the New International Version Old Testament; eighty-four of these are recorded in the Prophets – especially Ezekiel and Jeremiah. Today God still speaks to us by His Spirit. Theologically I had no problem with this, as the Scriptures are bulging with examples, from people like Joseph in Genesis to John in the Book of Revelation, but it had never been my experience until that night.

The dream

I woke up with a very vivid, full-colour movie picture of a beaver's dam. To the left of it the ground was dry and barren, with only a few trickles of water filtering through. Along their courses there was vegetation. On the right of the dam a large volume of water was being retained. I could see people on the dam itself, working in an attempt to dismantle it. I had a strong sense that they knew the water needed to be released, so that it could flow across the barren ground. I was equally aware they were, by and large, not being very successful.

I was then taken down under the water, which was being held back by the dam, to its foundations. There I saw a large log lying across the full length of it, with the words 'The Ulster Covenant' written on it. I clearly heard a voice speaking to me, 'If you want to see this water flow out across the land, then you must remove the log in the foundations of this dam.' The 'you' mentioned here had a very personal implication and also a wider corporate dimension to it.

My journey

It's at a time like this that I wish I had kept a personal diary. It would have enabled me to give you days and dates, etc., and therefore a more chronological order to my writing. But, it is sufficient to say that having had such a vivid image, I was unable to quickly brush it off. In fact, it has kept itself very much to the fore over the last eleven years in a lot of what I have been doing, first as Prayer Coordinator and now as the current leader of the community at the Christian Renewal Centre in Rostrevor, Co. Down, Northern Ireland.

The journey during these years has been punctuated by a number of 'stop-overs' at oases and a series of landmarks or milestones – not unlike the altars and stone pillars the children of Israel erected on their wilderness journey – firm reminders to them of specific meetings and encounters with God. It is these I want to share with you. Some of the chapters will have either a major historical or theological content to them, so 'hang in there' with me on the journey to my current place on that road (current, because it stretches on ahead of me into tomorrow). If, like me, you feel this is of God, then we need to journey together to see something happen, which has – as I have already mentioned – not only far-reaching consequences for Ireland, but also potentially for other nations!

The context of that vision is clearly the Ulster Covenant and the Home Rule Bill of 1912, and I now know that the water in that picture is the River of God (mentioned in Ezekiel 47, John 7 and Revelation 22) – the Holy Spirit – and that God longs for the day when the current Church leadership in the Presbyterian, Church of Ireland and Methodist Churches (along with the Congregationalist, Reformed Presbyterian and Baptist Churches, which I found mention of in my research) identify with the wrong actions of their forefathers in putting the Covenant in place, and dismantle it through repentance, thus enabling a mighty torrent of the Holy Spirit to flow. Keep that thought constantly in mind as I retrace my steps.

I am totally convinced that my forefathers' response to the Home Rule Bill was wrong. It may have been a different time in history, politically and spiritually, but in retrospect I believe that they were wrong. Their actions have had devastating consequences in Ireland and for our generation, since the late 1960s. Rick Joyner reiterates this in his booklet, *Overcoming the Accuser* when he writes:

> 'The church has had a long history of trying to bring the kingdom of God on earth by might and power, without the Spirit. But the Lord stated: *"That which is born of the flesh is flesh; and that which is born of the Spirit is spirit"* (John 3:5). Even if we are trying to accomplish the right goal, if it is not done by the Holy Spirit we will end up wounding instead of healing, bringing further division instead of reconciliation.'   (p. 58; para. 1)

If you were to ask me, 'Who am I writing this book for?' My answer would be for three specific groups of people:

1. Primarily, to provide information for the leadership of the main Protestant Churches in Ireland regarding the nature of a massive spiritual battle that we are currently involved in. The leadership of these Churches endorsed this Covenant in 1912 and they strongly encouraged the Protestant people to sign it. We need to understand afresh that by doing this Satan has actually been given power, which he continues to exercise in the realms of Irish politics and the Church. Covenants are legally binding and cross-generational in their effect. Repentance by the current leadership would be of tremendous help in the process of removing Satan's legal right to continue to exercise that power.

2. To give insight for the Christians of Ireland (and further afield in the Diaspora) who want to seriously intercede for Ireland – 'May Your Kingdom come, may Your will be done in Ireland, as it is in heaven.' So much of what we pray on a daily basis (and rightly so) is at a 'fruit' level, but I believe that what God has revealed here calls us to pray into the 'roots'. Jeremiah understood this when he writes, *'They have healed the wound of my people lightly, saying "Peace, peace," when there is no peace'* (Jeremiah 8:11 RSV). Cessation of violence does not constitute peace!

3. To encourage anyone around the world who has a heart for intercession, reconciliation or restoration issues, to be open before God to hear Him speak and to guide them in their researching of the historical issues that hinder His purposes for their nation.

Behind everything I want to share with you in this book is what I believe to be the heart cry of God, 'I want Ireland back and I want my Church back. You have made idols out of both and as a result you are unable to enter into all I have for you, the fulfilment of your destiny and calling as a people among the nations.'

Harry Smith
April 2006

The Ulster Covenant

The Solemn League and Covenant

Being convinced in our consciences that Home Rule would be disastrous to the material well-being of Ulster as well as the whole of Ireland, subversive of our civil and religious freedom, destructive of our citizenship, and perilous to the unity of the Empire, we, whose names are underwritten, men of Ulster, loyal subjects of His Gracious Majesty King George V, humbly relying on the God whom our fathers in days of stress and trial confidently trusted, do hereby pledge ourselves in solemn Covenant throughout this our time of threatened calamity to stand by one another in defending for ourselves and our children our cherished position of equal citizenship in the United Kingdom, and in using all means which may be found necessary to defeat the present conspiracy to set up a Home Rule Parliament in Ireland. And in the event of such a Parliament being forced upon us we further solemnly and mutually pledge ourselves to refuse to recognise its authority. In sure confidence that God will defend the right we hereto subscribe our names. And further, we individually declare that we have not already signed this Covenant.

God save the King.

CHAPTER 1

Uncovering the Past

So what do you do with an image like that? One thing was certain; because of the way in which it broke so forcefully into my life I couldn't ignore it. I had grown up in Northern Ireland, within the Protestant tradition, so I knew of the Ulster Covenant. But to be honest I was lacking in any great depth of detail or understanding, and as I was later to find out this was also the case of most Protestants I was to talk to!

I don't know how many of you have watched programmes produced by the Discovery Channel on television. I have watched with fascination a number of them showing an archaeological dig. As they go down through the different layers, more and more of the history of the region is exposed. It brought history to life for me in a way most history books have not. This chapter and the next one have been a bit like that for me – exposing the layers has given insight and understanding to the spiritual and political dynamics unfolding before us in Ireland today. So I started to research in articles, in books, on the web, cataloguing my findings as I went. In these two chapters I want to give an overview of some of them. Most of the information speaks for itself but I will make a few personal observations and comments at the end of Chapter 2.

In this chapter the insights into 1912 will probably be different from any others you may have ever read and the overview of history in Chapter 2 is most likely something you have not done in recent years. If you feel as I often have regarding Irish history, 'Oh no, not more!', then you may want to move on to Chapter 3. If you do, I would ask you to revisit these chapters at a later stage. At the risk of 'putting people off' the rest of the book, I have felt it necessary to start with them, not only because they are at the commencement of my journey but also because an understanding of the historic context is essential if you are to grapple with the direction the ensuing chapters take.

Before looking at the events of 1912, I will set the scene by going back to 1886 when the British Liberal Party first introduced the Home Rule Bill. It provoked a very hostile reaction from many shades of Irish Protestantism. Following special meetings of the Church of Ireland Synod, the Presbyterian Church's General Assembly and the Methodist Conference all parties produced resolutions, strongly critical of the Bill. The Methodist Church in its denominational paper wrote: 'Home Rule for Ireland means not only war against the crown rights of England, but against the crown rights of Christ ... its inspiration is religious antipathy, its methods plunder, its object Protestant annihilation.'

Alwyn Thompson, Research Officer for ECONI (Evangelical Contribution on Northern Ireland, now called the Centre for Contemporary Christianity in Ireland), wrote in an article entitled, 'God, Land and Nation: We will not have Home Rule':

> 'Protestant hostility was not only channelled through denominational structures. Mass rallies, which cut across divisions of denomination, class and politics, were organised in opposition to Home Rule. In 1892, 12,000 delegates met in Belfast for a great Convention. The meeting began with prayer from the Anglican Archbishop of Armagh, Scripture reading from a former Presbyterian moderator and the singing of a Psalm ... The demonstration of 1892 also revealed the breadth of Unionist

opposition to Home Rule. Liberals and conservatives in both politics and religion stood side by side. The Orange Order[1] was present, but only as one strand among the Unionist community. The organisers of the Convention, fearful that their opposition could be misrepresented as nothing more than sectarian prejudice, were well aware of the need to demonstrate the breadth and coherence of the Unionist position.'

On the other hand, the *Oxford Companion of Irish History* gives another slant to the issue:

'The most authoritative statement of what Home Rule meant was made by Isaac Butt (founder of the Home Rule Movement), who envisaged an arrangement whereby Ireland, Scotland and England would have a common sovereign, executive and "national council" at Westminster for the purposes of statehood in the international arena, while each country would have its own parliament for domestic affairs. In Ireland's case the specific form of parliament would be decided by an Irish assembly elected on the basis of household suffrage.' (p. 245)

This Bill failed to become an Act, as did a second one in 1893. It was with yet another attempt at introducing the Bill in 1912 that I will allow R. Finlay G. Holmes, former Professor of Church History at the Presbyterian Church's Union Theological College, Belfast, to take us further in the development of our understanding on those days. Here are some excerpts from his *Studies in Church History, Vol. 20, the Church and War*:

'[So] the crisis did not come upon the Unionists "as a thief in the night" ... from the beginning, their defiance was articulated and encouraged by leading prominent churchmen. On the eve of the general election of 1910 which brought the Liberals to power, eleven former moderators of the Irish Presbyterian Assembly took the unprecedented step of publishing a manifesto in which they contended that the best interests of all the people of Ireland were safeguarded by the union with Great Britain ... an independent Irish parliament, however would reverse this process and establish a Roman Catholic ascendancy with "clerical control" even in matters that were "purely civil and secular".

Protestation to the contrary by men like John Dillon[2] that "they would no more take their political guidance from the pope of Rome than the sultan of Turkey or conduct their affairs at the bidding of any body of cardinals", if they had even been heard, were not believed. The Moderator of the General Assembly of 1912, Henry Montgomery, an earnest evangelical ... declared that 'such promises and pledges are not worth the breath used in speaking them or the ink required to write them."

The Witness (the Presbyterian Newspaper), from the beginning of the home rule crisis, assumed an uncompromisingly Unionist stance, insisting that it was innocent of the "blasphemy as well as the arrogance" of associating God with one party rather than another, and admitted that "neither party is God's party" ... *The Witness* contended, it was because Home Rule would hinder the advance of Christ's kingdom in Ireland that it was being opposed.

On February 1st 1912 a convention of Irish Presbyterians was held in the Assembly Hall in Belfast, with overflow meetings in some inner city churches ... it attracted considerable support[3] from Presbyterians in general, and *The Witness* rejoiced in its unequivocal reaffirmation of the opposition to Home Rule previously expressed in 1886 and 1893. Some of the speakers who addressed the convention did not shrink from the ultimate implications of their position. T.G. Houston, Head Master of a leading Grammar School, insisted that no sacrifice was too great for their noble cause: "In the last resort they should be prepared to sacrifice even life itself rather than yield to what would prove the ruin of themselves and their country". He warned the government that their threats were not "empty vapour". They were made, not in jingo, but in a martyr spirit.

This Presbyterian convention received a message of support from the Church of Ireland Primate, Archbishop Crozier, assuring them that their action "in the present terrible crisis" would be followed by a similar demonstration of Anglican feeling. The vice-president of the Irish Baptist Union offered the convention his "heart-sympathy" and shortly afterwards Irish Methodists held a similar assembly to express opposition to Home Rule.

Undoubtedly many elements combined to make Ulster Protestants' resistance to Home Rule the implacable force it became – religious conviction and prejudice, economic self-interest, national consciousness and culture, perhaps even, as historian Joseph Lee has suggested, racialism. "Racialism, articulated in religious idiom, dominated Scotch-Irish hostility to Home Rule." The economic arguments of the Unionists, he believes, had racialist overtones, successful Ulster businessmen suspecting that the Celt was incapable of mastering the industrial virtues.

In 1912 Ulster Unionists, with the blessing of Protestant church leaders, were preparing to fight in the original words of Randolph Churchill "Ulster will fight and Ulster will be right." On Easter Tuesday in 1912, 100,000 men paraded at Balmoral ... in an impressive show of strength which began with a religious service led by the Church of Ireland primate and the Moderator of the General Assembly.

The Witness continued to pour out scorn on those who did not share the majority view that resistance to Home Rule, even in arms, was a sacred duty. An editorial in July 1912 read: "There are some who say that this is an unwise and unchristian attitude, that the prudent and Christian attitude should be for the Ulster Protestants to lick the rod and bite the dust and lie down and let the conquerors trample over them; better chains of slavery than resistance ... it is a peace at the price of freedom ... a peace at too great a price. For weal or woe it will not be paid."

The Witness Dublin correspondent wrote: "How can it be affirmed that we are transgressing the law of Christ? The New Testament does not teach nations the law of non-resistance any more than the Old. In 1690[4] our forefathers ... successfully fought our great battle for civil and religious liberty. What sort of spurious Christianity is this that tells us that we must not lift up a voice in protest or a hand in defence? God's witnesses in all generations cry shame on such a proposition."

F.E. Smith, hitherto little known as an authority on Christian ethics, was quoted as asking an assembly of Orangemen on the 12th July: "If we are not prepared to die for our faith, in the name of God and of men what is there we would die for?"

The fact that *The Witness* found it necessary to return again and again in editorial articles to the subjects of religion and politics, war and peace, suggests that there were still those who had not been convinced by their arguments. The dread implications of Home Rule were reiterated ad nauseam. It would reverse the revolutionary settlement of the seventeenth century on which their liberties depended. They resented accusations of bigotry and intolerance against them when they were only opposing the bigotry and intolerance of Rome. Their determination to resist was undiminished, "Unless the Cabinet drops its mad policy there can be no escape except in a baptism of blood."

The climax and supreme demonstration of the Ulster Protestants' determination was the signing of the Ulster Covenant on 28th September 1912, known as Ulster Day. The text of the Covenant was largely the work of the Presbyterian ruling elder, Thomas Sinclair, and recalled the historic Scottish covenants, which occupied a hallowed place in Presbyterian memories and imaginations. It was, Joseph Lee has suggested, "the traditional technique of reminding God whose side He was on". It pledged its signatories, "humbly relying on the God whom our fathers trusted ... to stand by one another in defending for ourselves and our children our cherished position of equal citizenship in the United Kingdom, and in using all means which may be found necessary to defeat the present conspiracy to set up a home rule parliament in Ireland." 237,368 men signed it and 234,046 women signed a parallel Declaration at over 300 centres throughout Ireland.'

Finlay Holmes also makes a few other comments on events in 1913, which give further insight into the hearts and minds of Protestants at that time:

'In 1913 at the celebration of the 300th anniversary of Irish Presbyterianism, a professor of history, addressing the meeting, said as his closing remark: "A great cloud of witnesses ... are looking down on this moment ... Let us be true to the heritage they have left us and not surrender lightly what they have won for us at so great a cost." Few of his hearers can have failed to understand his message.

Commenting on the annual Orange demonstrations of July 1913, *The Witness* applauded the Orangemen as soldiers preparing for battle: "How could men better die than facing the forces of Rome for the faith and liberty of their fathers, for the life and liberty of their children? There may be some who think this wanton and wicked. We would say that anything else is weak, cowardly and traitorous, we hope that history will never have to level these charges at the people of this generation who represent such a noble ancestry."'

Excerpt from *The Reformed Presbyterian Synod* – 2nd February 1912

The Synod passes unanimously the following declaration regarding Home Rule:

'That this Synod reiterates its condemnation of the proposal of the Government to grant what is called Home Rule to Ireland, as such measures would –

1. Violate to the uttermost the Solemn League and Covenant by which Great Britain bound itself to God in the year 1643;[5]
2. Make the "man of sin" the real king, or rather tyrant, of Ireland through the Irish majority . . . ;
3. Surrender the Protestant minority in Ireland to an admittedly and "conscientiously" murderous ascendancy;

4. Supply Jesuits with a new lever for fronting civil and international war in order to further the development of their fatal power, and the corruption, humiliation, and destruction of Protestant Britain.'

Excerpt from Bardon's *History of Ireland*

In the Ulster Hall they sang 'O God our help in ages past.' Then after prayer and lessons, the former Presbyterian moderator, Dr. William McKean, rose to deliver his sermon, taking as his text 1 Tim 6:20 *'Keep that which is committed to Thy trust.'* In it he declared: 'we are plain, blunt men who love peace and industry. The Irish question is at bottom a war against Protestantism; it is an attempt to establish a Roman Catholic ascendancy in Ireland to begin the disintegration of the Empire by securing a second parliament in Dublin.' (p. 437)

Excerpt from *Newtown: a history of Newtownards*

Services were held in First Presbyterian and the parish church an hour before the signing ... the Rev. Dr. Wright was the speaker. He outlined the dangers of Home Rule under which all power would be in the hands of one party, and invoked the spectre of the Catholic Church ... He referred to the Scottish Covenants and the role of covenants in the Bible and in history and urged his congregation to stand firm in defence of their rights, religion and liberties. Religion and politics were deliberately fused. The cause acquired the character of a crusade. D'Arcy, the bishop of Down, claimed that their opposition to home rule was 'essentially religious'. The moderator of the general assembly, Henry Montgomery, declared that it was not enough that religious services should accompany the signing of the Covenant. Prayer, he insisted, did not imply 'the discarding of the sword, it may only involve the strengthening of it'. Preacher after preacher at services throughout the province insisted that it was a religious, rather than a political occasion. (pp. 178, 179)

Excerpts from *The Ulster Covenant: A Pictorial History of the 1912 Home Rule Crisis*, edited by Gordon Lucy

Prelude

Unionists believed that any new Dublin Parliament would be predominantly Roman Catholic, and unduly influenced by that Church – hence the popular slogan 'Home Rule is Rome Rule' – and freedom of religious practice for Protestants would soon be drastically curtailed. To the Loyalists of Ulster it was not bigotry to try and prevent the setting-up of a parliament of bigots.

In an age when religious affiliation frequently determined political allegiance in Britain, the Unionist campaign against Dublin had the familiar ring of a religious crusade – one for the defence of Protestantism ... The emphasis on a common Protestantism rather than denominationalism proved an enduring bond which assumed, then and later, an immense political, as well as religious significance.   (p. 7)

The Leaders

To meet the danger the signatories pledged themselves to join 'In using all means which may be found necessary,' and that meant even the use of force.

As leader of the Ulster Unionists, Carson was the first to sign. Lord Londonderry representing the aristocracy and gentry, came next. The vital contributions of the Churches and of the Christian faith were recognised by the prominence given to the signatures of notable churchmen.   (p. 23)

The Document

The Presbyterians, with their tradition of sturdy independence, the very backbone of Ulster Unionism, were well acquainted with the concept of the solemn covenant in the religious history of Scotland in the sixteenth and seventeenth centuries.   (p. 43)

Religion

All over Ulster some 500 religious services were held on the morning of Ulster Day, bringing together representatives of all the Protestant denominations.

The *London Daily Telegraph* observed: 'The more strictly political objects of the Covenant derive all their strength and stability from this religious character.' The *Belfast News Letter* noted that: 'religion lies at the very foundation of the lives of the people.' Of Ulster Day itself the same newspaper declared: 'This was no occasion for demonstration, but for dedication to a higher purpose.'

The religious dimension was reinforced by the sturdy display of support for the people's actions on the part of the Protestant Churches. Charles Frederick D'Arcy, then Bishop of Down and Connor and Dromore and later Archbishop of Armagh, summed up the position of Christians in the crisis when he declared 'we hold that no power, not even the British Parliament, has the right to deprive us of our heritage of British citizenship.'

Before the signing of the Covenant started in Belfast, a religious service was held in the Ulster Hall with representatives of the Presbyterian, Anglican, Methodist and Congregational Churches all participating. This and all the other services throughout Ulster reminded everyone present of the solemnity of their commitment in signing the Covenant.

All over Ulster religious services were held on Ulster Day before the signing of the Covenant. A standard service sheet was produced for such gatherings ... The moving spectacle of Ulstermen uniting together in one mind and with one purpose before their God inspired the production of many poems, songs and hymns. One example, published in 1913, identified Ulster's struggle for survival with the struggle of the ancient Israelites. There is a covenant between God and His people, but it is a covenant which requires that the favoured people keep faith with God: 'And of the cup our fathers drank, give us the strength to drink.'

(pp. 53, 54, 56, 58)

The Sequel

In the words of the seventeenth century philosopher Thomas Hobbes, 'Covenants without swords are but words.'

Carson realised that it was not enough to preach the use of force without making practical preparations to acquire the means ... With Carson's unequivocal support, Major Frederick Crawford (who had signed the Covenant in his own blood) in a daring mission travelled to Germany, purchased guns and ammunition and brought them safely to Ulster. On the night of 24th April 35,000 rifles and 3,000,000 rounds of ammunition were successfully unloaded at Larne, Bangor and Donaghadee and swiftly and efficiently distributed to the UVF[6] right across the Province. Ulster now not only had the will but the means to oppose the imposition of Dublin rule. (p. 90)

The excerpts that I have quoted above have all been collated and written years after the events surrounding 1912. I now want to give you some quotes from the *Belfast Newsletter* (a major daily Protestant Newspaper in Northern Ireland) in 1912, which told its readers about the story as it was unfolding. It gives us a powerful insight into the hearts and minds of the editor, the clergy and the politicians at that time. Some of it I found extremely sad and painful to read.

I quite literally spent days in the Linenhall Library in Belfast, going through micro-film of the *Belfast Newsletter*, where I photocopied many articles, some of which I have given below. Others are in the appendix at the end of the book.

Excerpts from the *Belfast Newsletter*

8/7/12: A vigorous sermon by Rev. Dr. McDermott

Preaching last evening to a large congregation in Belmont Church, the Rev. Dr. McDermott, who chose as his text 1st Kings, 18th chapter, 21st verse, said it was a special doctrine and a special tradition that had led him to say that Home Rule was Rome Rule. In one of his best-known books, Cardinal Newman asserted that the chief doctrine of Rome was her doctrine of the Church, which meant the sole supremacy of the Pope over the Church of Christ, and his infallibility. The contention which was used in medieval times to express the Papal claim was that St. Peter in the garden received two swords. One of these was the spiritual power, and the other was the temporal power, giving him and his successors control over kings and kingdoms and the persons of their peoples and their secular affairs generally. These medieval Popes believed that they were vested by Almighty God with power to depose sovereigns, to release nations from their allegiance to them, to order the murder or assassination of disobedient persons, and to reward and approve those who perpetrated them.

It gave one pause to think that if the Home Rule Bill were to become law, the most influential men in the country would be the Hibernians – men who would have no crown and no King, and no British people and no Protestantism. He wished to suggest, however, that it was neither right nor fitting at the present time to set up a system of reprisals, blind, squalid, and indefinite, as those reprisals were sure to be. No doubt, the provocation was great, especially when already feeling was greatly strained, but Protestants stood for the law of the land and an orderly resistance, if it must come to resistance. It might be said on that point that no Christian man was compelled by any just law to hold his life and liberties, the welfare of his family, and the fruit of his industry at the mercy of the Church of Rome. Passive resistance might suit the conscience of the individual – he (the speaker) did not judge him – but it did not suit large bodies of men. He thought it was Hugh Miller who said that in Europe, Protestantism behoved to fight for its life or it never would have continued to live. That seemed true. In Germany, in Switzerland, in the Netherlands, in England in the days of Queen Elizabeth, in the three kingdoms in the time of James II, religious liberty required to be protected by arms and men.

To him the present crisis was of the greatest gravity, as fateful in regard to Protestantism as anything that had happened since the Apprentices hastily closed the Gates of Derry and kept out the soldiers of King James. But because the peril was so extreme, every care must be taken to exhaust all peaceful remedies. He did not believe that the Home Rule Bill would ever receive the signature of his Majesty if Irish Protestants were found faithful in the calamity that threatened them, if they were roused out of their supineness to give time and money for the next two years so that the eyes of the British Protestants might be opened. Therefore, he said, let them abandon these domestic squabbles, this civil war in a street or in a factory; let them 'trust in God and keep their powder dry.' God was not dead. Providence was ever ruling, and would not refuse their prayers.

8/7/12

An impressive service was held at Bangor yesterday afternoon under the auspices of the local district of the Loyal Orange Institution. It had been announced to be held in the Methodist Church, but when that place of worship had been filled it was found that there was a very large number of people unable to gain admission. The meeting was conducted by the Rev. William Maguire. In the course of an appropriate sermon, which was based upon Ephesians 6 v. 11 – 'Put on the whole armour of God', Rev. William Maguire referred to the critical times through which the Protestants of Ireland were passing, and the danger which lay ahead, emphasising the importance of Unionists being united throughout the country in order to resist the encroachments of Rome, and urging them to be loyal to Jesus Christ and the teaching of the Bible.

11/7/12: *An important letter from Sir Edward Carson* (*London, 9th July 1912*)

My dear Colonel Wallace – In view of the approaching celebrations of the Twelfth July[7] it is of supreme importance that every care should be taken that the lodges and other persons taking part in the celebrations should assist their leaders in preventing disturbances or breaches of the peace. I quite understand the intense state of feeling caused in Ulster by the conduct of the Government in expressing its determination to force a Home Rule Bill upon the people of Ulster and the unalterable determination of Ulster to resist such proposals, and I am also conscious of the great provocation and indignation caused by the recent conduct of the Ancient Order of Hibernians.[8]

I desire, however, to point out (and I feel certain you will agree) that self-control and discipline and the preservation of the peace are essential at the present time, and that any rioting or disturbance, which are at all times to be deprecated, can only lead to mis-apprehension and disastrous consequences. Our friends may rest perfectly satisfied that when the proper time comes, all necessary steps with proper organisation will be taken to assert our position and safeguard our interests.

Yours sincerely,
Edward Carson

According to the British Broadcasting Corporation's website[9] Edward Carson:

Was born in Dublin, into a liberal professional middle class family and studied law at Trinity College. He was amongst the most successful lawyers of his generation. The reputation he acquired led to his election as Unionist MP for Trinity College (1892–1918), and to his becoming Solicitor-General for Ireland (1892), and for England (1900–05). In parliament his speech attacking the Second Home Rule Bill in 1893 was widely acclaimed; he had emerged by 1906 as one of the most prominent politicians in the United Kingdom.

In February 1910, Carson agreed to become leader of the Irish Unionist Parliamentary Party and in June 1911 accepted Craig's invitation to lead the Ulster Unionists. He brought credibility and prestige to the movement. His objective throughout was to preserve the union between Britain and Ireland, believing it to be in the best interests of his fellow-countrymen; he was an Irish patriot, but not a nationalist. During the home rule crisis, 1912–14, he aimed to foment and use Ulster's resistance as a means of blocking any granting of self-government to Ireland. Owing to his undoubted charisma, inspired oratory and unyielding image, he was hero-worshipped by unionists in the province of his adoption. Carson was deeply uneasy about the decision to establish an Ulster Volunteer Force and to run guns through Larne. However he accepted them as a means of applying additional pressure to the British government and so reaching the negotiated agreement he privately sought. By 1914, he had come to support Irish partition as a solution, fatalistically accepting that Home Rule was inevitable. By then his strategy had brought Ireland close to civil war. His image is that of an intransigent unionist leader who helped raise the political temperature in Ireland and bring it to the brink of civil conflict. However, he himself felt a profound sense of unease about the measures then being taken by his supporters in Ulster.

14/7/12: *Report on Sermon by Presbyterian Moderator on 'Rome and Religious liberty'*

Speaking last night in the Shankill Road Mission's large Albertbridge Hall, the Right Rev. the Moderator of the General Assembly (Dr. Henry Montgomery) said there was no one more strongly convinced than he was that the great function of the Christian minister was to proclaim in all its length and breadth and fullness the unsearchable riches of Christ. Nor was there anyone more fully persuaded that what was known by the name of politics should not be discussed in the pulpit. And yet it seemed to him that even (if) he endeavoured to stir public opinion towards some great temperance reform he was introducing a political theme. A very grave outlook, however, confronted them at this time, in the presence of which everything else shrank into insignificance. The Protestants of this country were face to face with a danger which threatened them with the loss of everything which they held dear.

Some people might call any reference to the proposed grave political changes now before the Houses of Parliament a political matter. That word failed to describe it by a long way. To him, at any rate, the proposed legislative changes had within them the gravest danger to their civil and religious freedom. He could not conceal from himself that the Roman Church stood to gain everything by the proposed legislation, and the Protestants of the country, as far as man could see, stood to lose everything which they valued. It was not pleasant to have to speak of these things, especially when multitudes of their people had had friendly relationships with their Roman Catholic fellow-countrymen, and had no personal ill-feeling against them; but as they were face to face with changes which were calculated not only to damage their religious institutions, but ultimately, in many parts of Ireland at any rate, to extinguish the evangelical lights that had been burning there, he could not keep silent and be fair to his own convictions and true to evangelical religion in this land.

It was very well known that there was no 'live and let live' with the Roman Church. Her policy from time immemorial, which had never changed, was a policy of extermination where that was possible ... Their birthright was that they were sharers in the great British Constitution – the home of civil and religious freedom – that this was their inalienable right, and within that Constitution they meant, by the help of God, to live and die. Nothing could shake them from that stern determination ... Their position was that they should have full, free, and unfettered liberty to preach the Gospel of the blessed Lord in every part of the land; an open Bible, and an unfaltering adherence to the great principles of civil and religious liberty which they had enjoyed throughout the centuries that were gone. They had no ascendancy, and they wished for none, but they would not have anyone else practise ascendancy over them.

Whilst adhering to their religious convictions they were quite prepared to live in friendly relationships with their Roman Catholic fellow-countrymen. That had been the attitude of their Church all through the past. Their people had suffered severely since they settled in this land nearly three centuries ago, and they suffered in Scotland and resisted to the death any interference with the liberties which they enjoyed … The country might be more or less asleep today as to the real aims of the Roman Church in regard to this land, but the day of awakening was at hand. He counselled them to put in practice the toleration, forbearance and patience which were associated with the gospel of their Lord and Saviour. He wished that prayer might abound, and that they might supplicate Almighty God to come to their deliverance once more and prove to them again, as He had proved in the past, that He heard and answered prayer. The language of the ancient Psalm was still true of His Church: 'God is in the midst of her; she shall not be moved. God shall help her, and that right early.'

29/8/12: Letter from Rev. George R. Wedgwood to the Editor

Sir – A goodly number of people have asked me if the Methodists are not going to take part in the proposed religious services in relation to the very grave national crises through which we are passing, and I wish to say that so far as I can persuade them they will.

An unnecessary political measure is being forced upon the country, which has awakened in the hearts of hundreds of thousands of our countrymen the most painful fears. They may be right; they may be wrong; but they are there. We need to be reminded that still 'God is our refuge and strength, a very present help in trouble.' Only His interposition can avert the threatened calamity. It is the pressing duty of all Christian people to pray, both in public and in private that He will give our senators wisdom and the people self-control, and that He will save the country from civic strife.

2/9/12: Ballymena District Black Chapter Demonstration
at Randalstown – Part of the preparations for Ulster Day –
A test for Unionists

Mr. W.H. Webb, J.P., proposed 'That we again affirm our reasoned determination never to submit to a Nationalist Government in Ireland, and on Ulster Day we are prepared, in proof of our determination, to sign our names to that document which will go down to posterity as "The Solemn League and Covenant of the Protestants of Ulster" '. They had, he said, again and again, affirmed their opposition to Home Rule and their determination never to submit to a Government which would be dominated by the Ancient Order of Hibernians; but now they were asked to affirm their resolve in a different way – in a way which would make it plain to the people of England and Scotland that they were in earnest. Six months ago the situation was very critical; but, thank God, the dawn was now breaking. He could see it coming; and he did not believe that Home Rule would ever be forced on Ireland. He did not say this in order to make them slacken their efforts to defeat the Bill now before Parliament; he simply said it because he had confidence in the manhood of Ulster – in the Protestantism and the Protestants of Ulster. Come what might, he believed they were determined never to submit to be governed by the Ancient Order of Hibernians, the head of the Roman Catholic societies in this country. The Loyalists of Ulster had at the present time the best leaders that any crisis had ever produced.

Proceeding, the speaker said they were determined not to have Home Rule; they were born under the British Constitution and under the ruling Sovereign of the United Kingdom, and they were not going to change their allegiance for a monarch who lived at Rome. No foreign ecclesiastical potentate would ever be allowed to rule over the Protestants of Ireland. That was their determination, and they were prepared to fight and die for it if necessary, as their forefathers did at Derry, Aughrim, and the Boyne. Who wanted Home Rule? ('Nobody at all') It was not the Protestants of Ulster or the farmers throughout Ireland, be they Roman Catholic or Protestant. The people who wanted Home Rule were the members of the Ancient Order of Hibernians and the other scum of the country.

2/9/12: Reports

The Very Rev. the Dean of Dromore, in an eloquent and effective speech said they had been reading in some newspapers about the rowdy and rebellious Orangemen, but the men who wrote such articles know nothing about the Order. The loyalty of Orangemen was not a thing of yesterday. They accepted a condition of things by the settlement of 1688, and they meant to stick by that condition of things, and if necessary suffer for their resolution. At present the Ship of State was in the hands of pirates but by God's help, it would shortly be under different masters. The action to be taken by Ulster in a short time would compel the British electorate to think, and the reverses the Radicals were now suffering at the polls would be followed by others of a still more paralysing description. The folds of the Union Jack were wide enough to shelter and protect all who were now under them, and it was the intention of Irish Loyalists to live and die under them.

Rev. R. Andrews (Donaghadee) speaking at a Co. Down Rally, said with him Home Rule was a religious matter. It was a question of Popery or Protestantism. Popery meant a closed Bible, superstition, and bondage; whereas Protestantism stood for liberty and freedom and for salvation through the cleansing blood of Christ.

He held that it was against the laws of nature that men who had once known freedom and liberty could ever again be brought back into bondage. The soul of Ulster had breathed the air of civil and religious liberty, and Ulster could never again return to bondage and superstition, to the bidding of Popery and the priest.

5/9/12: Part of Editorial

The Pastoral which the Lord Primate and Bishops of Derry, Kilmore, Down and Clogher have addressed to the members of

the Church of Ireland in the Province of Ulster is a proof that they
take a grave view of the present political situation. They state that
we are face to face with a great crisis in our religious and political
history, and that 'momentous changes are proposed for the future
government of Ireland, the disastrous consequences of which, if
carried out, none of us can forecast.' When the ambiguous
phrases of the Home Rule Bill are put into the briefest and
clearest terms, its object is seen to be the conversion of Ireland
into a Roman Catholic State, and the subjection of its Protestant
inhabitants to the control of the Vatican.

The members of the Government profess to believe that
Protestants have nothing to fear, but the truth is that they do
not care what becomes of them, and their sole object in making
their reassuring speeches is to persuade the British public that
their bill is not a blow to Protestantism as well as a constitutional
outrage. Is there any sane man who believes that it makes no
difference to the Protestants of Ireland whether they remain
under the Imperial Parliament, in which there will always be an
overwhelming majority of Protestants, or under an Irish Parliament in which the Roman Catholic majority will be equally
overwhelming and permanent? Let the Radicals, if they can,
name any Roman Catholic country in which Protestants have
been given equal rights, or one in which they enjoy equal rights at
present . . .

If the Bill passes, they are to be subjects of the new Papal State,
bound to obey laws which they will have no share in making, and
to pay whatever taxes their Romanist conquerors choose to
impose. The sovereignty of the King will be purely nominal. He
will be represented in Ireland by a Roman Catholic Lord
Lieutenant, who will drive in State through the streets of Dublin
to High Mass, perhaps accompanied by a Papal Legate; who will
take precedence over him. His Excellency will act on the advice of
a Roman Catholic Prime Minister, who will be responsible to a
Roman Catholic Parliament, which will in turn be subservient to
the Roman Catholic hierarchy . . .

16/9/12: *From an Editorial*

It is more than two and a half centuries since the Scottish Covenant was signed in the Churchyard of the Grey Friars at Edinburgh amid a tumult of enthusiasm. This was indeed but the solemn renewal of that which had been sworn to in a previous hour of peril, when Great Britain lay under the shadow of the threatened Spanish Armada. 'We promise and swear', were its concluding words, 'by the name of the Lord our God, to continue in the profession and obedience of the Protestant religion, and that we shall defend the same, according to our vocation and the utmost of that power which God has put into our hands, all the days of our life.' Gentlemen and nobles rode with the document over the country, gathering subscriptions to it and, from every side, the people pressed in to sign. Circumstances certainly have changed since those far-off times, and watchwords which provoked enthusiasm then fail to stir men today; but the principle which lay behind the signing of the Scottish Covenant remains unchanged. In a free country men still refuse to bend to the autocracy of a Monarch or a Cabinet.

17/9/12: *From an Editorial*

Now that the active anti-Home Rule campaign in the Imperial province leading up to Ulster Day has begun, Unionists all over the North of Ireland are preparing to do their part in the great historic demonstrations which are to be held in different important centres. Ulster has been the scene in various periods of her history of stirring political events. In the stricken field of battle, in the initiation of great patriotic movements, with courage, and unflinching determination, her people have filled many a notable page in history but, on the present occasion, Ulster Day will be the apotheosis of a spirit of dauntless resolve which for intensity of purpose has never been equalled. The people of the province have united heart and soul in the determination to resist Home Rule by every means in their power. That they are in earnest is irrefutable and indisputable. In the most solemn manner they will subscribe their names to the Covenant, the prototype of which was that issued in 1643 for 'the defence of religion, the honour and happiness of the King, and the peace and safety of the Three Kingdoms of Scotland, England and Ireland.'

The movement which culminated in that League had its origin in the civil conflict between Charles the First and his Parliament; the one to be signed on Ulster Day has its genesis in the action of the present Radical Government in forcing through Parliament by unconstitutional methods a measure of Home Rule which legitimately inspires every Protestant and lover of his country with dismay and dread. The terms of the Covenant have not been disclosed, but briefly it will be a declaration to the effect that the signatories will never consent to be ruled by a Home Rule Parliament, never recognise its laws or pay the taxes it levies. Never was there a greater slander uttered than that Ulster was weakening in its opposition to Home Rule.

18/9/12: Mr. F.E. Smith. KC. MP. Part of a speech given at a Unionist Meeting in Spa, England

'I am going with other Unionist members to Ulster to take part in the great series of meetings which will lay down, in language more serious than has been used by any great body of subjects to the sovereign power of these realms since the Revolution of 1688, what is the determination of the men of Ulster. Let nobody make the mistake of thinking that we are going in any spirit of levity; or with any disposition to attenuate that responsibility which we and other public men take in joining our voices in that campaign of protest which will begin then.

Let there be no mistake either about what we shall urge the people to do, or about what the people there are going to do. They are going to say – with a full knowledge of all that it involves, with a complete realisation of the steps, active and passive, to which they may ultimately be driven if the wickedness of the Government carries it so far – what the Duke of Abercorn said nearly twenty years ago – "Whatever the consequences may

be, we will not have Home Rule." All religions, creeds and
political creeds are entering into a League and Covenant the like
of which, for solemnity and for binding force, has not been
witnessed in English history since the first "Solemn League and
Covenant", the memory of which is one of the most cherished
possessions of the Scottish people.'

18/9/12: Part of Lord Carson's speech, Enniskillen

'We warned the Government, and we told them that we stood
where the men stood in 1893 – that our motto was the same, and
that we would not, and we will not, have Home Rule. Yes,
and then you remember we followed that up with the great
meetings of all the Churches who, thank God, are one upon this
great question. I suppose one of the most remarkable demonstrations that has ever taken place was the meeting of the
Presbyterians in Belfast, when some 35,000 members of that
Church came there and filled every hall, and in the presence of
that God that they serve, announced their determination for the
protection of their civil and religious liberties. The Methodist
body did the same, and the Church of Ireland passed resolutions
to exactly the same effect. And then we wound up with the great
meeting at Balmoral, at which I know many of you were present.

What effect has all that upon the Government? Why, they
have treated it as so much empty frothing and boasting; they have
paid no heed to it. What do they care about the Protestant
Churches in this country; what do they care about the community of Presbyterian, Church of Ireland, and Methodist?
Nothing at all; they only care about the English Nonconformist
conscience, which for its own purpose and largely to its shame is
prepared to desert its fellow co-religionists in this country for
political and party purposes. They have waged war upon the
most law-abiding people and the most faithful constituents of
the United Kingdom. What are we to do under these grave and
responsible circumstances? Does anybody advise us to surrender?'
('No', and cheers).

21/9/12: *Part of an Editorial*

And if the Protestants of Ulster now fail to do their duty, or shrink from the sacrifices which they may be called upon to make, they will prove unworthy of their race, and betray the cause for which brave men have always been content to fight and to die. If a Roman Catholic Parliament is set up in Ireland, Papal rule will follow and everyone knows that it has always been, and still is, inconsistent with civil and religious liberty, and a menace to every Protestant citizen.

23/9/12: *Mr. F.E. Smith. KC. MP. – Speaking at a Demonstration in Ballymena*

I do not believe that there is a man or a woman who on Ulster Day will sign the Covenant, who will not be proud for the whole of their lives that they were privileged to put their names to a document which, I believe, will be the seal of your national and your Protestant liberties. And let no one underrate the binding and the solemn force of those great national memories. But for how long have you lived? For how long have you fed the dreams of the patriotism of your youth out of that deep well which inspired the Battle of the Boyne?[10]

For more than two hundred years you have refreshed your own courage, and you have educated and inspired your children in the memories of that battle. But you cannot live forever, however glorious that may be, on the memories of your ancestors. It is time for you, listen to me, to make history for yourselves, to hand down to those coming after you – and I am satisfied that, with a deep sense of individual responsibility, every man and woman will sign that covenant on Ulster Day. I make this final prediction to you that, in days to come, when you and I may be followed to our fathers, many a child in Ulster, enjoying the fruits of your labours, it may be the result of your devotion in cherishing the precious heritage of full civil and religious freedom, will say, 'My ancestors won them for me long ago at the Battle of the Boyne and, in a more recent day, by those who rallied around Carson and signed the Solemn League and Covenant of 1912.'

24/9/12: Rev. J.W. Gibson, at a Unionist Meeting at Dunmurry
'The Loyalists of Ireland would never submit to be ruled by a Parliament in Dublin controlled and engineered as it would be from Dublin. The spirit of the men who fought at Derry, Enniskillen, Aughrim and the Boyne was with them still, and, if need be, the men who would subscribe their names to the Covenant on Saturday would be ready should the exigencies of the situation demand it to shed their life's blood in defence of faith and fatherland.'

Excerpts for the *Belfast Evening Telegraph*

24/8/12

ULSTER DAY.
MEETING OF CLUBS' COUNCIL.
THE SIGNING OF THE COVENANT.

A meeting of the Unionist Clubs' Council was held yesterday in the Unionist headquarters at the Old Town Hall, Belfast – Mr. E. Slater, J.P., in the chair. There was a large attendance of delegates.

A large amount of business in connection with Ulster Day was transacted.

Captain Craig delivered an address, in which he referred to Ulster Day, which, he said, would be a solemn and serious day in the province. The event would be one of the most important in Irish history. The Covenant would be signed by many thousands of loyal men and women. Its full text would be made known in due course. It has been carefully considered by Sir Edward Carson, who would be the first to sign with Lord Londonderry at noon on 28th September. They need not place any reliance on the rumours that the Government would proclaim the meetings.

It was announced that meetings should be held in as many localities as possible, the details being left to the local committees representative of the clubs, the Orange Institution, Women's Unionist Clubs, and Unionists generally, the committees to report to headquarters.

With reference to the services it was stated that they were to be locally arranged.

The meeting ended with the singing of 'God Save the King.'

11/9/12: Ulster Day, Presbyterian Appeal

Attitude of the Church
Important Pronouncement

The Continuation Committee appointed as the result of the Presbyterian Convention on 8th February last, has issued the following manifesto – To the Ministers and People of the Presbyterian Church in Ireland.

Representing, as we do, the Continuation Committee of the Presbyterian Convention held February last, and by way of giving still further effect to its aims and decisions, we venture to appeal once more to our Presbyterian brethren, throughout the country.

The proposed observance of Ulster Day on Saturday, September 28, and the announcement of the arrangements for its celebration add emphasis to the fact that the struggle against Home Rule has now reached a more acute and intensified stage, which renders it necessary that the united Protestantism of the country should reaffirm, with even greater determination than ever, its opposition to a policy which seeks to inflict upon us intolerable injury and injustice.

We have always maintained that the question of Home Rule is one which transcends mere party politics. To establish a Dublin Parliament which would be controlled by that Church which has lately promulgated in Ireland the *Ne Temere*[11] and *Motu Proprio*[12] decrees, and in which Protestants would be in a helpless minority, is a policy which threatens religious freedom, endangers the rights of conscience, substitutes a religious ascendancy for our present religious equality, and strikes a deadly blow at the Protestantism of this country. Not only would our religious liberties be gravely imperilled, that we should be deprived of our British citizenship; thrust out of our position in an empire to whose greatness we have been ardently loyal, and to whose greatness we have contributed our full share: and should have our political future and our material interests transferred to the control of a Parliament which we profoundly distrust.

In these grave circumstances we regard with the strongest approval the proposal to set apart a portion of Ulster Day for the worship of God. We therefore earnestly recommend that services be arranged for in all our churches, or where owing to circumstances this may not be possible that united services be held, and that all our people assemble to take part in them. In our judgment the services should begin with humiliation and confession of national sin and shortcomings. They should embrace intercessions for our leaders that they may continue to have Divine guidance; for our people, that they may act as becomes the children of an historic Covenant, and do nothing unworthy of its great memories; and for our countrymen of all creeds and opinions, that distrust and suspicion of each other may be dispelled, and that they may learn to unite in mutual effort for the promotion of the best interests of Ireland. They should include prayer to Almighty God that in His all wise providence the course of events and counsels of statesmen may be so overruled that the dangers which threaten our land may be averted, and a happy deliverance vouchsafed from all our fears. Facing the present crisis in this spirit, we shall be able to subscribe to the Ulster Covenant in the faith and courage of our fathers, and to leave the issue with their God and ours.

Signed by authority of the Continuation Committee.

Thom. Sinclair, Chairman	R.H.F. Dickey, D.D. Hon. Sec.
John Young, Vice-Chairman	William McKean, D.D.
William Crawford, Treasurer	Robert Smyth
S. Law Wilson, D.D. Hon. Sec.	William Smith
John Stewart, D.D. Hon. Sec.	

Notes

1. See note at the end of Chapter 8.
2. 'Dillon was the Nationalist Party's most accomplished parliamentarian ... his vision of Irish nationality was broad and liberal. Earnestly Catholic, he opposed clerical leadership in politics' (*The Oxford Companion on Irish History*, p. 148).
3. The *Witness*, Special Supplement for Friday 2nd February stated that '40,000 tickets for admission to the various meetings were issued.'
4. See note 10.
5. This in an inaccuracy – the Solemn League and Covenant in 1643 was a covenant made by the Scottish Reformation Covenanters against the Crown.
6. UVF. The Ulster Volunteer Force was founded in 1912 by Sir Edward Carson to fight against Home Rule. Many UVF men joined the 36th Ulster Division of the British Army and died in large numbers during the Battle of the Somme in July 1916. Fifty years later the current UVF was formed, taking the name and symbols of the original UVF, to combat what it saw as a rise in Irish nationalism centred on the 50th anniversary of the 1916 Easter Rising. It had the express intention of executing 'mercilessly and without hesitation' known men in the Irish Republic Army (IRA). (*Source*: Adapted from the BBC's website – http://www.bbc.co.uk/history/war/troubles/factfiles/uvf.shtml)
7. See note 10.
8. Established in 1836 in New York. In Ireland and Britain it was still small until after 1900. It was Catholic and broadly nationalist. The Belfast Nationalist leader Joseph Devlin (national president of the Order from 1905–34), turned it into a political machine for the Nationalist Party. It was attractive to businessmen for its freemasonry-style activities, to workers for its benevolent activities and to young Ulster Catholics as a rival to the Orange Order. (*Source*: *The Oxford Companion to Irish History*, p. 13.)
9. *Source*: http://www.bbc.co.uk/history/war/easterrising/profiles/po02.shtml
10. No year in Irish history is better known than 1690. No Irish battle is more famous than William III's victory over James II at the River Boyne, a few miles west of Drogheda. James, a Roman Catholic, had lost the throne of England in the bloodless 'Glorious Revolution' of 1688. William was Prince of Orange, a Dutch-speaking Protestant married to James's daughter Mary, and became king at the request of parliament. After being ousted, James sought refuge with his old ally, Louis XIV of France, who saw an opportunity to strike at William through Ireland. He provided French officers and arms for James, who landed at Kinsale in March 1689. William

could not ignore such a threat and countered it by coming to Ireland himself, to quell any possible resistance.

The Battle of the Boyne is recalled each July in the celebrations of the Orange Order, not on the first day but on 'the Twelfth', for eleven days were lost with the change from the Julian to the Gregorian calendar in 1752. (*Source*: *A Little History of Ireland* by Martin Wallace.)

11. *Ne Temere* (literally meaning 'not rashly' in Latin) is a decree (named for its opening words) of the Roman Catholic Congregation of the Council declaring invalid any marriage of a Roman Catholic or any person who has ever been a Roman Catholic, unless contracted before a qualified Roman Catholic priest (or the bishop of the diocese) and at least two witnesses. The decree was issued under Pius X, 10 August 1907, and took effect on Easter 19 April 1908. (*Source*: http://en.wikipedia.org/wiki/Ne_Temere)

12. A document issued Motu Proprio is from the Pope *on his own initiative*, and not in response to a request or at the initiative of others. Its legal determinations carry the full force of papal authority, though it does not derive from existing laws unless specifically stated. (*Source*: http://www.secondexodus .com/html/catholicdefinitions/motuproprio.htm)

CHAPTER 2

Many Layers, Much Pain

Maybe you are not like me, but I have a habit of putting things down, even putting them away and then forgetting where I have put them. This is made worse by the fact that when I do need them, it is usually in a hurry. This invariably results in a mad scurry around the house in a frantic search. Eventually, when I calm myself down and in a controlled way retrace my steps, I usually have success in finding where I put them.

Retracing our steps is not always that easy, and especially when it comes to history. I started the last chapter in 1886 when the British Liberal Party introduced a Home Rule Bill, but I soon began to realize that this was only part of a trail that went back centuries. Thankfully, things like microfilm of the *Belfast Newsletter* of 1912 were full of clues. In them the speeches of clergy and politicians gave me a number of clear footprints of people and events in the sands of time. There were two definite paths that I found I needed to walk down, one here in Ireland and the other across that narrow strip of water to Scotland and England. And so often these ancient paths appeared to criss-cross each other. As in Chapter 1, this is not a definitive history – there are many histories out there, each with their own insights and interpretations. What I am attempting to do is put into some sort of spiritual and historic context the happenings of 1912.

I woke up early one morning, while I was writing this, with a very strong sense that God was saying to me 'On reading this chapter you need to have a "devotional" approach to the history outlined here' – that your hearts should be open to the heartbeat of God. I have become so painfully aware of the layer upon layer of events that all the people of this island have had thrown at them, down through the centuries. Aware also that, *'our struggle is not against flesh and blood, but against the rulers, against the authorities, against the powers of this dark world and against the spiritual forces of evil in the heavenly realms'* (Ephesians 6:12). God has put an apostolic anointing on this land that is manifested in the missionary endeavours that have flowed out from here since the times of St Patrick and the early monastic/missionary endeavours, causing thousands to come out of Satan's kingdom into God's kingdom of light. We also see this manifested in the depth of compassion and the capacity to care that is within us, as Irish people. This is shown in many social and practical ways, as we have reached out into the needy places of this world.

Satan has hated this so much and has sought with an incredible level of success to distort this calling, especially over the past 400 years since the plantation. The history written here is not written from the perspective of 'pointing the finger', 'blame shifting' or 'people group bashing', but rather I sense God wants us to grasp something of His heart in the following pages. He wants to redeem, heal and restore at this time. We do not need to allow this pain to continue down into another generation. I firmly believe that is why He wants the negative power of issues like the Ulster Covenant dealt with.

A few years ago Bill Roy and Brendan McCarthy made a contribution towards peace on this island with an initiative called 'The Alternative'. Part of that contribution was a helpful little booklet, a sort of 'canned history' of Ireland, which I have dipped into, as a chronological and informational guideline in writing this chapter. In it they wrote:

'...in our pasts, our communities have imposed themselves on one another, at times ousting other communities from the land (Vikings, Normans, English, Welsh, Scots, French, Dutch, Spanish to name a few). We are all here now; that doesn't mean to say that any of us got here without trampling on those who were here before us. The long-lost pre-Celtic inhabitants of Ireland were the only people to occupy an empty land; we must all admit that our origins as well as parts of our histories owe too much to oppression. Equally, we must all be gracious in forgiving those who have oppressed us ... this is not the easy way, but it is the way of the Kingdom of God.'

Sowing seeds of division

I do not want to spend too much time in going back to the times of St Patrick (mid-fifth century) and the introduction of Christianity to Ireland. Yet even back then seeds of discord were being sown. Patrick, a Roman citizen, favoured the Diocesan system of governing the Church, while the growing leadership in the Irish Church was establishing a Church based on independent monastic settlements. Through time a growing conflict appeared between the Celtic and English Churches, coming to a head with the Council of Whitby in AD 664 where a decision had to be made over calculating the date of Easter. This was foundationally an issue of authority (sounds familiar!). In the end it was the king, not the church leaders, who made the decision – an indicator of an increasing, though not always healthy, relationship between Church and State, and also paving the way for ongoing difficulties in relationships between the Irish and English kings and the English Church and the papacy. Canterbury also became the headquarters for English Christianity and it was also around this time that a debate resurfaced as to whether or not its jurisdiction should extend into Ireland. This forced the Irish Church and political leaders together under the umbrella of Irish Church independence. The stage was set! Seeds of division were sown!

In the eleventh century, during the times of the Viking presence in Ireland, the jurisdiction of Canterbury was recognised, with the Archbishop consecrating the Archbishops of Armagh and Dublin. The twelfth century saw Henry II, an Anglo-Norman, invading Ireland, to quell the potential threat of fellow Anglo-Normans there, like Strongbow, who were becoming increasingly more powerful. The intertwined relationship between Church and State continued to unfold as Adrian, the English Pope, recognised Henry II as Lord of Ireland and gave him authority to carry out ecclesiastical reforms there. On the basis of this, Henry invaded Ireland to take control of the situation. The Bishops accepted his lordship in return for Canterbury being denied jurisdiction over the Irish Church, which, on regaining its independence, made Armagh the ecclesiastical capital of Ireland – which it is to this day.

Fast forwarding to the fifteenth century, we find England embroiled at home in the War of the Roses and also intermittently warring with France. It seemed that as long as Ireland was not opening up another battlefront, England was happy enough to leave well alone. In 1494 the War of the Roses was over, Henry VII was on the throne and he decided to exert his influence on the Irish stage by forming a parliament in Drogheda. It was only to meet with his approval and could only pass laws that he and his council agreed on. Overall Henry VII was happy to have his rulership over Ireland conducted through appointed Irish families, such as the Fitzgeralds. By the time Henry VIII came on the throne however, Spain had emerged powerfully on to the scene and Ireland's loyalty had to be secured to ensure it was not used by Spain as a back door into England. And also, for personal and political rather than spiritual reasons, Henry had broken with Rome.

The Reformation

In 1541 a 'Reformation Parliament' made Henry King of Ireland and also the 'Supreme Head on Earth of the Whole Church of Ireland', outlawing anyone who proclaimed the Pope to be the head of the Church. He was prepared to give back land to any Irish or Old English lords who accepted these conditions. His successors – Edward, Mary and Elizabeth – though not necessarily having the same religious convictions, continued with the English colonisation process. The conquest of Ireland reached its peak under Elizabeth when in 1560 the Irish Parliament's Act of Supremacy made her the head of the Irish Church. This was followed by The Act of Uniformity, which tried to enforce compulsory church attendance with The Book of Common Prayer being the only liturgy to be used in worship. While it was not possible to enforce this Act, it introduced a terrible equation into the situation: to be Protestant was to be loyal to the English crown and to be Irish was to be Catholic. Much worse was to follow, during the seventeenth century, which is to this day seared into the corporate memories of our divided communities.

The Plantation

It began with 'The Flight of the Earls'. This was a voluntary exile of more than ninety of the Ulster Chiefs, who chose to leave their ancient kingdoms rather than stay as landlords subject to the English crown. James I used this situation to begin his policy of plantation, during which 'profitable land' was given to English and Scottish settlers – also known as planters.[1] While this process was a rather complex one, it nevertheless left a defensive settler population that was loyal to the crown and an Irish population that was full of resentment.

During the middle of this century, Charles I was increasingly at odds with the English Parliament, and the country moved towards civil war. The Old English (of Norman descent) joined forces with the remaining Irish leaders and sided with the crown in an attempt at gaining favour and better conditions from the King. On the other hand, most of the Protestants in the Irish Parliament, along with most of the Ulster settlers, sided with the Parliamentary forces.

In 1641 there was a rebellion in both Dublin and Ulster, and one of the worst atrocities during that year, done with the backing of the Catholic Bishops, was the drowning of hundreds of Protestant men, women and children in the River Bann near Portadown.

1642 saw a trail of events: leading Catholics set up a provisional government in Kilkenny (the Confederation of Kilkenny); the Parliament in Dublin expelled its remaining Catholic members; the King, wanting to keep the support of the Irish Parliament, sought to make a truce with the Confederation; this was misinterpreted by many Protestants who thought the King was sympathetic to the Catholics; and the Catholic Bishops and leading Catholic laity declared the 'insurgence' war against the 'Puritans' to be a just one. The following year, a truce with the King only served to further the Protestant alienation with the crown.

Cromwell

The Civil War ended with the execution of Charles I, and Oliver Cromwell coming over to Ireland to restore English Parliamentary control, in 1649. He saw this as something of a spiritual as well as a military crusade, claiming: 'We came, by the assistance of God, to hold forth and maintain the lustre and glory of English liberty in a nation where we have an undoubted right to do it.' In both Drogheda and Wexford his victorious troops showed no mercy, slaughtering the besieged inhabitants, 'avenging' the 'slaughtered saints' of 1641. During the 1640s it is estimated that over 500,000 people were killed (one third of the population). Such a loss through political and religious violence has left a deep wound in Ireland's psyche.

Cromwell's victories also saw further plantation in Ireland, which was to continue even after the restoration of the monarchy. Scottish settlers also continued to pour into Ulster, boosting the Presbyterian population. Between 1641 and 1665, Catholic land ownership had decreased from 60% to a mere 20% – most of that being in the impoverished West.

When James II, a Catholic, became king, he allowed Catholics to hold important offices in Ireland once more. This served to open up old animosities and suspicions of the 1640s once again. He too had his conflicts with the Parliament, which eventually led to the Dutch William of Orange becoming England's co-monarch with his wife Mary. His time in Ireland, while blessed by none other that the Pope himself, has mostly been seen as a Protestant victory over the Irish Catholics.

By the time we enter the eighteenth century, Ireland was divided into three fairly distinctive people groups: a dispirited and dispossessed native Irish people; an English Administration with an ever expanding population of English settlers, and thirdly, in Ulster the Scots planters who were clearly making themselves feel more and more at home. For the English this was always a potentially explosive mix, and keeping the Irish in place appeared to be the best solution.

Penal Laws

This was done by a series of harsh Penal Laws which included excluding Catholics from:

- Parliament and voting
- the legal profession
- teaching
- carrying arms
- buying land. Catholics who did own land were not allowed to pass it on to the eldest son, but rather had to divide it equally among the male heirs.

The Penal Laws also affected Presbyterians – they were also denied the vote; their marriages were not recognised by the State and they were required to pay tithes to the Church of Ireland. One of the major effects of these laws was a dispersion of many Catholics and Presbyterians to Europe and America.

As the eighteenth century progressed developments like the American War of Independence and the French Revolution played a dominant role in spawning the idea of an Irish Republic in the hearts of many Catholics, Presbyterians and a few members of the ascendancy, in which they could be united under a fair and equal governmental system. In 1782, under Grattan's leadership, an Irish Parliament was granted, giving them a limited notion of nationhood. Though separate from the English Parliament, they were still under the Crown.

Any ideas of furthering that dream were shattered by old rivalries between Catholics and Protestant planters re-emerging in Ulster, but yet at the same time, in other parts of the island Catholics and Presbyterians were still collectively exploring the idea of a Republic. In 1791 the formation of the United Irishmen saw the birth of Republicanism. Wolf Tone, who is widely regarded as a founding father of Irish republicanism also became known as the father of the 'physical force' tradition – the use of armed struggle. An attempted rebellion in 1798 was ruthlessly crushed, with most of its leaders being executed. From this a new ideology of republicanism was birthed, with 'armed-struggle' becoming an intrinsic part of it. The Irish Parliament was dissolved and the Act of Union in 1800 created the United Kingdom under a single Westminster Parliament.

The Great Famine

During the early 1800s, the liberalising influences of The Enlightenment were instrumental in the voices of Catholics and liberal Protestants being raised regarding Catholic emancipation. This was attained under the leadership of Daniel O'Connell, resulting in the repealing of the Penal Laws in 1829, though the confiscation of the Catholic land during the Penal Law time was to have disastrous consequences in the middle of the nineteenth century, when Ireland was struck with the Great Famine. A population of over eight million people, predominantly poor rural dwellers, was decimated when for two years in a row the potato crop failed. During the first year the government aid was poorly administered and in the following year a new government adopted a policy of non-intervention – starvation, typhus and exposure took their toll: one million people died and a further one million risked the 'coffin ships' as they fled to America.

Not surprisingly, the famine left its mark deep in the psyche of Irish Catholic people, regarding the British administration. Further attempts at revolution fizzled out and it took the emergence of the Nationalist Party under Parnell, towards the end of that century, to firmly establish constitutional nationalism in Ireland. Perhaps, not surprisingly, this produced a strong reaction from many Ulster Protestants. When the British Government made several attempts at introducing the Home Rule Bill, the stage was being set for stiff resistance by 'whatever means necessary' to be formalised in the Ulster Covenant of 1912. And so we are back around to Chapter 1.

Yet another layer – the Scottish Covenanters

Studying history with my spiritual eyes and ears open has given me a fresh love for history – well, some of it anyhow – particularly, when it is linked to intercession for the Ireland of today and our need to be liberated from the spiritual bondages imposed upon us by past negative actions of our forefathers.

I was not very far into my research of the Ulster Covenant before I noticed that links were being made (in the *Belfast Newsletter* and the Presbyterian magazine, *The Witness*) to Ulster Presbyterian roots in Scotland, and in particular to the Scottish Covenanters. Insight into the theological and political thinking in Scotland in the early 1600s is therefore needed to enable us to understand something of the Protestant mindset, not only in the Ulster of 1912 but also today. The Website of the Grand Orange Lodge of Ireland[2] even takes us back to an older Scottish Covenant in 1580. As most of the other documentation of events in 1912 takes us to 1638 and 1643,[3] it is there that I will commence this overview.

Scotland's 'Marriage with God'

For many Scots, Wednesday 28th February 1638 was 'The glorious marriage day of the Kingdom with God'. Many of Scotland's noblemen (and probably hundreds of lairds) assembled in Greyfriars Church in Edinburgh, where they signed the document, which was soon to be known as the 'National Covenant'. In the weeks that followed copies of the Covenant were signed with enthusiasm, and sometimes by force, in many parts of the country. In many cases clergy, during church services, exhorted all present to swear to uphold the Covenant. Some leading covenanting nobles and lairds also carried copies around and had people sign it in their home districts or shires.

This revolt of the Covenanters can be seen as arising from the long-term consequences of the two most important turning points in the country's history, in the previous century:

1. The Reformation, which gave Scotland a Protestant Reformed church saw Scotland reject her traditional alliance with Catholic France. This national independence, which triumphed hand in hand with that of Protestantism, was closely linked to national issues regarding their identity as Scots.

   Scots Calvinists saw themselves as part of the universal true Church of God. From 1560 onwards, these ideas were revived and intensified into the boast that the Church of Scotland was the best reformed church in the world, an example to others. Scotland might be a small and poor nation but, mysteriously, she had been specially favoured by God to be a model for others. The way was thus prepared for the development of the idea of Scotland as a nation with a special 'covenanted' relationship with God.

2. The Union of the Crowns. England had intervened militarily in Scotland to establish a Protestant regime free from French control. In the ensuing turbulent decades, this intervention (diplomatic and military) sustained the regime.

As soon as the young King James VI of Scotland came of age, he made a formal alliance with England and accepted an annual pension from Queen Elizabeth of England. As a result Scotland was in grave danger of becoming a client state. Two circumstances made the situation bearable – the two nations were now bound together by both having adopted Protestantism, and politically a momentous development was on the horizon. King James VI was the heir to the childless Queen Elizabeth, though she would never openly confirm his right to the English throne. Fears about Scotland's political dependence on England were therefore allayed by looking forward to a Scottish king taking over the English throne – he would preside over this link and, surely that would provide protection for the smaller kingdom in a Britain united under one sovereign.

Protestantism and the fear of Catholicism pulled the two countries together. Yet, on the other hand, the different variants of Protestantism, which ultimately triumphed north and south of the border, pushed the two apart, emphasising their separate identities (Calvinist versus Episcopalian).

Because of the dynamics mentioned above, conflict began to develop in the 1570s. Religion was too powerful a force for religious autonomy to be acceptable to the state: as in many other Protestant countries, the crown argued that the ultimate earthly authority in religion, which had been wrested from the Pope, must be taken over by the sovereign, as God's representative on earth, if royal power was to be maintained.

In Scotland Presbyterianism emerged, which claimed that the spiritual jurisdiction of the Church there was entirely separate from the secular jurisdiction of the State. There were 'two kingdoms' in Scotland, and the civil had no power within the ecclesiastical one. Presbyterian zealots often seemed to regard their spiritual kingdom as superior to that of the State. It was the State's duty to help the Church when asked, and it was the Church's duty to show the civil powers (including kings) how to perform their duties in godly ways. This implied the superiority of the Church.

The revolt of the Netherlands against the Spanish Crown in the 1560s was of great interest to the Scots, both because they had close commercial and cultural ties with the Netherlands and because Calvinism had emerged as the ideology legitimizing the struggle of the Dutch against Spain. Interestingly, just as the Dutch brought this covenantal thinking to South Africa to become the theological foundations of the apartheid regime, so the Scots brought it to Ulster during the time of the plantation.

Further historical insights

In 1636 a new Book of Canons, or codes and regulations, was imposed on the Church of Scotland. Two aspects of the book caused particular unease: the book was largely a reprint of an earlier English Book of Canons and it was imposed on the Church by a royal prerogative. A new Scottish Prayer Book was also drawn up, and like the Canons, it was based on its English counterpart. The Scottish Church was not only being anglicized, it seemed to be officially accepted that its Church was subordinate to England's, and that an English Archbishop had a right to a leading role in its affairs.

Finally, not content with meddling with Church government, discipline and worship, King Charles I added interference with basic theological beliefs. For many Scots, the writing was now on the wall for their Church. The piecemeal reform of religion in Scotland by James and Charles, now seemed to a great many Scots, and not just a few fanatics, to be leading inexorably back to Catholicism.

Their response was the National Covenant of 1638. It was a band or bond – a written and signed agreement or contract. The vast majority of bands were purely concerned with local and regional relationships. However, in times of crisis, the signing of collective bands (which could be religious as well as political) could be a method of consolidating a faction at a national level, those who signed agreeing to stand together for a common political purpose.

Still to take place were theological developments, which were to provide another ingredient of the National Covenant – the idea of special relationships with God, defined in covenants. The Hebrew words usually translated as covenant occur in the Bible several hundred times, and are used to describe agreements, explicit or implicit, defining the relationship between God and man, or more particularly between God and His chosen people, the Jews. Through such biblical references, the idea of compacts between God and man had long had a place in Christian theology, but usually a fairly marginal one. In the late sixteenth century, however, some Calvinist theologians began to give the covenant idea a central place in their teachings, resulting in the development of what became known as 'federal' theology through use of the Latin word *foedus* for covenant – a word which could also be translated as 'contract' or 'treaty'.

And so a twist developed

Through possession of the best reformed Church on earth, the Scots saw themselves as in a sense the successors to the Jews, clearly chosen by God, awarded a unique status. The unique relationship with God must therefore be a covenanted one, for God had had special covenants with the Jews. Thus covenant ideas heightened the nationalistic element present in the Church in Scotland, particularly in those inclined to Presbyterianism. For them Scotland was a chosen nation, the Scots an elect people with a great role to play in God's dispensation. Moreover, being a chosen people, specially favoured by God, put the Scots under particular obligations. If it was sinful for any people to accept corrupt religious practices such as those imposed by James VI and

Charles I, it was far more sinful for the Scots to do so. As a chosen people, their defection was the greater, the necessity of doing something about the situation to avert God's wrath all the more urgent. Moreover, surely this meant that once the Scots did start doing God's will, the unique status God had bestowed on them, the unique covenanted obligations He had undertaken to them, would give them victory, whatever the odds.

Some idea of what the Covenant meant to so many ordinary folk in Scotland is conveyed in the words of John Fleming, Session Clerk of the parish of Galston, Ayrshire: 'In thankful remembrance of the singular mercie of God who was pleased to receave this land into covenant with himself, more formallie than any other people we hear of since the rejecting of his old people the jews . . . '

Signing the Covenant, symbolizing Scotland's coming home to God and being received into His special favour, was a highly emotional occasion. With God's help, little Scotland was well on its way to destroying the power of the great King Charles I throughout all the kingdoms of Scotland, England and Ireland. The Chosen People were on the march.

These are pillars of remembrance historically, not particularly pleasant ones, but they stand there in history, shaping us today. So much of it, to my shame, I did not know before, but I need to periodically revisit them. They are very personal pillars of remembrance for me – speaking of times when God met with me and shared His heart regarding our collective history in ways which were at times deeply and profoundly painful.

Some personal thoughts

In all of my gleaning through the historical reference books, national daily newspapers and the denominational newspapers of the Presbyterian, Church of Ireland and Methodist Churches, I could not find anything suggesting that any of the churches need to actually revoke the Ulster Covenant, as they did not actually endorse it at a central governmental level within any of the churches. None of them officially opposed the Covenant at the time, though individual members did bravely express opposition. The Presbyterian Church, after examination of the text, put forward changes to the wording of the Covenant hoping to ensure that it was only to be applied to that particular time and not binding to subsequent generations (which we now know was not to be the case!). The text of the Covenant was also submitted to the other Protestant Churches for approval, which they duly gave. The Churches, therefore, were fully complicit in the crisis of 1912.

The *Belfast Evening Telegraph* of the 24th August recorded the Ulster Unionist Council's endorsement of the Covenant at a meeting the previous day and on the 11th September it reported the Presbyterian Church's strong support regarding the Covenant (see end of Chapter 1). The theology behind it is Scots Covenanter/ Plantation/Presbyterianism in origin. The wording of it was drawn up by Thomas Sinclair, a leading Presbyterian elder and Chairman of the Continuation Committee which was appointed after the Presbyterian Convention in February.

In talking to a number of key people within the Presbyterian Church, the understanding seems to be that Thomas Sinclair, along with other central political figures in the Ulster Unionist Council, initiated the whole proceedings of the day and that the majority of people, with the encouragement of the major Protestant Churches leadership, fell into line. The whole overall tone of the sermons, political speeches, newspaper articles of leaders in the churches and in politics were I am sure, very instrumental in procuring that.

My belief is that these churches need to acknowledge the role their predecessors played in not only providing the theological framework for the Covenant but also that through sermons, letters to the press and their own denominational papers, they used their position of authority and influence to encourage people to sign it. For that there is a need to own the sins of their fathers just as we read Nehemiah did in the first chapter of his book. I also believe it would be importantly significant if Christian politicians within Unionism could do likewise.

As I read the accounts of events leading up to the signing of the Ulster Covenant there were several things that disturbed me greatly:

- The way Protestant leadership (both political and spiritual) used fear – articulated through the press, their speeches and preaching – to communicate the errors of the Catholic Church from their Reformed Faith perspective.
- I had a sense that they were ultimately afraid of losing political power. These communications mentioned above were also used as a powerful tool to unite the Protestant community politically, against the Westminster Parliament's intention regarding the Home Rule Bill.
- Alongside these there was also I believe, a real fear of being a minority group swallowed up by a majority who were vastly different religiously, politically and culturally and as a result they would have become a voiceless group of people, no longer in the driving seat. Behind this was an underlying insecurity, one that continues to this day and which can be seen in the themes on the wall murals and flags which look back to our Scottish Covenantal roots. It betrays that our security is not truly in God. We have made Him a lesser god, an idol, and attached Him to the other idols we have made of the land and our nationality. This stands in opposition to the command of God – '*You shall have no other gods before me*' (Deuteronomy 5:7).
- I believe that the seditious and treasonable activity of gun-running and of also putting a provisional government in place was a gross act of rebellion against the British authorities. We are told in the Scriptures that as Christians we are to be in submission to the authorities over us (Romans 13:1, 5). Nowhere in the teaching of Jesus, his immediate disciples or Paul, do we read that such actions were ever taken against

the Roman authorities of their day. They recognised the spiritual nature of what was happening in the physical world (Ephesians 6:12).

- The British Empire. In retrospect, many aspects of empire building are radically wrong – conquering other people groups, taking their land, stealing their natural resources and suppressing their ethnic identities – all of which were often by force and in the name of God. I believe that God made all the ethnic groups in the world, each with their own special cultural richness, giftings and identities and that He has given to Britain a 'fathering' role among the nations of the world (just as Ireland seems to have been given an apostolic and compassion ministry in the world, as seen in our missionary and mercy ministry endeavours around the world, something more akin to the role of a mother). If this was, however, distorted by Satan, then it became control, power, suppression and authority rather than something that is serving, protecting and releasing. Today, God is raising up a growing number of ministries around the world, including groups like the English Reconciliation Coalition, to under-stand their history, recognise their wrongs and reach out to the people groups their forefathers have wounded, in acts of repentance and reconciliation, e.g. to the Irish Catholics for the wrongs of Cromwell and to the Australian Aborigines who were suppressed in the early dates of colonialism there.

As you read on, the good news is that our next stop is at an oasis. And what a watering hole! And so, with this information of the last two chapters to hand, let us go there . . .

Source material _____

An Introduction to Irish History by Bill Roy and Brendan McCarthy.

The Covenanters – The National Covenant and Scotland by David Stevenson (Saltire Press, 1988, Edinburgh).

The Scottish Covenanters by Johannes G. Vos (Crown and Covenant Publishers, 1940, Pennsylvania).

Notes

1. The planters were predominantly Scottish, bringing with them their distinctive Calvinistic/Presbyterian or Reformed theology with its central covenantal emphasis.
2. http://www.grandorange.org.uk/history/Fight_For_Union.html
3. 1638 – the Scottish National Covenant and 1643 – the Scottish Solemn League and Covenant.

CHAPTER 3

The Plumb-line

A few months into this journey, I was reading in my own personal daily devotions from the Old Testament book of Amos. In chapter 7 verses 7–9, I read:

> 'This is what he showed me: The Lord was standing by a wall that had been built true to plumb, with a plumb-line in his hand. And the LORD asked me, "What do you see, Amos?"
>
> "A plumb-line," I replied.
>
> Then the Lord said, "Look, I am setting a plumb-line among my people Israel; I will spare them no longer.
>
> > "The high places of Isaac will be destroyed
> > and the sanctuaries of Israel will be ruined;
> > with my sword I will rise against the house of Jeroboam." '

As I prayerfully reflected on this, I sensed the Holy Spirit was speaking to me from it regarding the whole issue of the Ulster Covenant and, in particular, the word 'covenant'. He showed me that the teaching on covenant from the Scriptures was His plumb-line. It was against this that He measured all other beliefs and understandings on covenant, to see if they were plumb or not.

To my shame I have to confess that I had, up to that point, not had any in-depth (never mind foundational) teaching on what God had to say about this. What a rich path of discovery I was to embark upon. Indeed, I would liken it to a fresh water spring, a welcome oasis in the desert (again, a very significant place for Israel as they journeyed to their Promised Land), one to which I would continually return, to ponder upon and drink from. The bottom line is that God's dealings with man have always been on the basis of covenant. To begin to understand this and to embrace it is to put our lives on an incredibly sure foundation. Our capacity to trust Him fully and to rest in Him flows out of this. Set up your tent here for a while, pull up a chair and let's have a drink.

What I want to share with you now has been brought together from a number of sources – commentaries, books, teaching tapes – most of which I have no record of, regarding title, author, etc. One small booklet however, which tied a lot of this together for me is *Explaining Covenants* by Tom Marshall (published by Sovereign World). I am much indebted to him for the concise way he presented the many strands of thought in the Scriptures.

Throughout the whole of the Bible God relates to people by means of covenants (sometimes called treaties or pacts). He is a covenant-making and a covenant-keeping God. Our hope and security as Christians depend entirely upon God's faithfulness to the promises He made in the Old and New Covenants (Testaments) and on our ability to appropriate and enjoy the benefits of these Covenants, through our continued responses of repentance, faith and obedience. Grasping the true nature and significance of our covenant relationship with God unlocks the meaning of many passages of Scripture and transforms our understanding of the nature of our relationship with Him.

At the heart of God's covenants is His desire to have a relationship with us. In fact, we were created to have an intimate relationship with Him. When Adam and Eve sinned, they broke covenant. *'Like Adam, they have broken covenant – they were unfaithful to me there'* (Hosea 6:7). Thankfully, God did not leave it there, but He began His redemptive search to restore our broken relationship with Him. This restoration was all embracing, because God wanted every area of our lives to know His wholeness – physical, moral, spiritual, intellectual, emotional – in our life vocation and in our relationship with each other. He wanted it to extend to the temporal and the eternal; the spiritual and the secular; the private and the public. In the world of today when so many people are looking for a sense of identity, security and belonging, it can be found in ever-increasing measure as we embrace the truths regarding covenant.

Three aspects of covenants in Scripture

There are three aspects of a covenant found throughout Scripture:

1. I will be your God (Genesis 17:7–8)
2. You shall be My people (Exodus 6:7)
3. I will dwell in the midst of you (Exodus 29:45–46)

Leviticus 26:12 states these three aspects:

> *'I will walk among you and be your God, and you will be my people.'*

As do other scriptures:

> *'I will establish my covenant as an everlasting covenant between me and you and your descendants after you for the generations to come, to be your God and the God of your descendants after you.'*
>
> (Genesis 17:7)

> *'You are standing here in order to enter into a covenant with the LORD your God, a covenant the LORD is making with you this day and sealing with an oath, to confirm you this day as his people, that he may be your God as he promised you and as he swore to your fathers, Abraham, Isaac and Jacob.'*   (Deuteronomy 29:12–13)

' *"The time is coming," declares the* LORD,
  "when I will make a new covenant
with the house of Israel
  and with the house of Judah . . .
This is the covenant that I will make with the house of Israel
  after that time . . .
I will put my law in their minds
  and write it on their hearts.
I will be their God
  and they will be my people." ' (Jeremiah 31:31, 33)

*'For we are the temple of the living God. As God has said: "I will live
with them and walk among them, and I will be their God, and they will
be my people." '* (2 Corinthians 6:16)

Covenant relationships are binding

The Hebrew word for covenant is *b'riyth*, which means 'to bind'.
Covenant relationships are mutually binding, and as we will see
later, are also confirmed by a solemn promise and an oath. The
classic biblical examples of this are between two people, such as
David and Jonathan: *'And Jonathan made a covenant with David
because he loved him as himself'* (1 Samuel 18:3); Laban and Jacob:
*'Come now, let's make a covenant, you and I, and let it serve as witness
between us'* (Genesis 31:44) and between a husband and a wife: *'For
this reason a man will leave his father and mother and be united with his
wife, and they will become one flesh'* (Genesis 2:24). They can also be
made between people groups e.g. Israel and the Gibeonites: *'Then
Joshua made a treaty of peace with them to let them live, and the leaders
of the assembly ratified it by oath'* (Joshua 9:15), and between God
and man. A key word in all of these is **faithfulness**.

Let us, for a moment, concentrate on the last expression of
covenant I have mentioned – between God and man – for it has
one key distinctive. Mark Buchanan in his book *The Holy Wild*
(Multnomah Press, 2003) writes:

'Through Abraham, He chose a people for Himself, a people to walk in His ways, live by His grace, trust His word, display His character. He *promised* all this. But here's the rub: **He guaranteed the promise by His own faithfulness**, not Abraham's ... It needed God's faithfulness.

The story is told in Genesis 15. To establish the promise, God *cuts covenant* with Abraham. This was an ancient ritual, in which the covenant partners hewed an animal in two. The severed pieces were laid out facing each other, a pathway marked between. The partners of the covenant walked this pathway, between the bloody halves of the carcass. This was to enact two things: a pledge to walk within the bounds of their promise, and a willingness, if they didn't, to suffer the same fate as the animal, to be hewn and scattered.

Always, both partners walked the pathway.

Except in this instance. Here all the other elements of cutting covenant are in place – the promise, the halved animal, the two pieces laid out, a pathway between. Only this time, just one covenant partner walks the pathway: God alone does.

The covenant, the vastness of its promise, depends on God alone.'   (pp. 59, 60)

It is the serious nature of 'cutting' the covenant that really strikes me. They entered the covenant by death, which the sacrifice represented. They gave up their rights to live any longer for themselves. They acknowledged that they had to die to their rights and from then on, live for and if needs be, die for the other party of the covenant. Whatever the other partner needs or asks for, they will supply. How light we make of this in our western society today, in issues like marriage. For so many people, including Christians, we enter into a covenant, but we treat it like a contract.

This is reiterated and expanded upon in Genesis 17:3–8:

'Abram fell face down, and God said to him, "As for me, this is my covenant with you: You will be the father of many nations. No longer

will you be called Abram; your name will be Abraham, for I have made you a father for many nations. I will make you very fruitful; I will make nations of you, and kings will come from you. I will establish my covenant as an everlasting covenant between me and you and your descendants after you for the generations to come, to be your God and the God of your descendants after you. The whole land of Canaan, where you are now an alien, I will give as an everlasting possession to you and your descendants after you; I will be their God."'

In the Abrahamic covenant the promise to Abraham and to his descendants is inseparable from God's promise of the land. Just as the seed of Abraham is ultimately extended to include those who believe in Christ, so too is the land promise extended. '...*Abraham and his offspring received the promise that he would be heir of the world*...' (Romans 4:13). Yet even with our being 'grafted in' to the olive tree which is Israel, God's relationship with Israel regarding nationhood and land still remains – His promise regarding these was never revoked or superseded: it was an everlasting covenant. It is also good for us to remember that, like us, God did not choose them because they were special; they are special to God because He did the choosing.

Other aspects of the nature of God's covenant with man

Because it is God's initiative, His gift to us, it is founded and maintained entirely on the basis of grace. It is completely undeserved: there is nothing in us that gives us any claim on His attention whatsoever. It is an expression of God's generous, forgiving and gracious character. In fact, it is within the context of covenant that God's character is most fully revealed:

'And he passed by in front of Moses proclaiming, "The LORD, the LORD, the compassionate and gracious God, slow to anger, abounding in love and faithfulness, maintaining love to thousands, and forgiving wickedness, rebellion and sin."   (Exodus 34:6–7)

At the very core of this verse is the Hebrew word *hesed*, constantly used in the Old Testament when speaking of the love of God. It can also mean 'steadfast love' or 'everlasting kindness'. It is linked to His faithfulness to the covenant bond:

> '. . . He is God, the faithful God, who keeps His covenant, and His lovingkindness [hesed] to a thousandth generation with those who love him and keep His commandments.'
>
> (Deuteronomy 7:9 NASB)

As already mentioned, it is God as the stronger party who sets out the conditions under which the covenant obligations will be fulfilled. He alone sets the terms. For our part, we can accept or reject them, but they are not open to debate or negotiation.

> 'Then he [Moses] took the Book of the Covenant and read it to the people. They responded, "We will do everything the LORD has said; we will obey." '
>
> (Exodus 24:7)

This is a very important principle for us to understand. One of the main reasons for not entering into the blessing of our covenant relation with God is that we have considered the terms too demanding for us. As a result we tend to try and side-step them, partially obey them or make attempts at offering to God something which is more amenable to us.

Another fascinating insight regarding the power of covenant is found in Joshua chapter 9. The Israelites were duped into making a covenant with the Gibeonites. It says in verses 14–15:

> 'The men of Israel . . . did not enquire of the LORD. Then Joshua made a treaty of peace with them to let them live, and the leaders of the assembly ratified it by oath.'

Verses 19–20 continue:

> 'We have given them our oath by the LORD, the God of Israel, and we
> cannot touch them now . . . We will let them live, so that the wrath will
> not fall on us for breaking the oath we swore to them.'

Fast-forwarding ourselves on a few hundred years to 2 Samuel
21:1–3 we read:

> 'During the reign of David, there was a famine for three successive years;
> so David sought the face of the LORD. The LORD said, "It is on account
> of Saul and his blood-stained house; it is because he put the Gibeonites to
> death."
>
> The king summoned the Gibeonites and spoke to them. (Now the
> Gibeonites were not a part of Israel but were survivors of the Amorites;
> the Israelites had sworn to spare them, but Saul in his zeal for Israel and
> Judah had tried to annihilate them.) David asked the Gibeonites,
> "What shall I do for you? How shall I make amends so that you will
> bless the LORD's inheritance?" '

A wrong covenant had been entered into, yet when it was broken
many generations later, God held them accountable for it and
judged them for it. The power of covenant lives on – for blessing
or for evil – transcending the generations. What our forefathers
did through the Ulster Covenant in 1912, and the Sinn Fein
covenant in 1916, still has incredible spiritual power today. If we
do not understand this, then we ask the question I have so often
been asked – 'What has that got to do with me? That was my
grandfather who signed it!'

Most importantly of all, covenant provides the means whereby we
can have a relationship with a holy God. It deals with the problems
of sin and obedience. The New Covenant, sealed with the blood of
Christ, is God's ultimate provision for us.

The nature of the Covenant bond

I have already touched on this when I quoted Mark Buchanan –
covenanted relationships are the most serious and solemn of all
relationships. Let us now explore why this is so. There are three
major steps involved in making a covenant: a promise, an oath and
a sacrifice.

A promise

A promise – the commitment of covenant – is basically an
undertaking to do or to give something to someone. Equally, it
can be an undertaking to not do or give something in the future.
It is not just a proposal or an intention: it is saying, 'I am making a
serious and earnest commitment as to how I am going to act in the
future. I intend that commitment to be taken and relied on and I
will act in the way I have declared. I am also taking on myself an
obligation to fulfil my pledged word. I am acknowledging that I
am limiting my freedom of action in that particular situation,
making myself duty bound to do or to act exactly as I said I would.'
In Psalm 89:33–34 we read:

> '. . . I will not take my love from him,
>   nor will I ever betray my faithfulness.
> I will not violate my covenant
>   or alter what my lips have uttered.'

What wonderful news!

Yes, God takes His promises very seriously. When He makes a
promise, He has committed Himself to that course of action, and
we are meant to take His promise as a pledge or guarantee that He
will do exactly what He has said. Paul, in writing to Titus puts it
this way:

> '. . . the knowledge of the truth which is according to godliness, in the
> hope of eternal life, which God, who cannot lie, promised long ages ago.'
>
> (Titus 1:1–2 NASB)

An oath

An oath is a further confirmation of the covenant, giving it an even greater seriousness or solemnity. The person is not only calling on God to bear witness to his words but he is also saying, 'I hold myself answerable and accountable to God.'

> 'Men swear by someone greater than themselves, and the oath confirms what is said and puts an end to all argument.'
>
> (Hebrews 6:16)

They are acknowledging that their honour and reputation is at stake. Even to this day, in a court of law, the making and breaking of an oath would make us guilty of perjury.

God's covenants are based on His promise confirmed by an oath:

> 'Then Joseph said to his brothers, "I am about to die. But God will surely come to your aid and take you up out of this land to the land he promised on oath to Abraham, Isaac and Jacob.'   (Genesis 50:24)

> 'You are standing here in order to enter into a covenant with the LORD your God, a covenant the LORD is making with you this day and sealing with an oath, to confirm you this day as his people, that he may be your God as he promised you and as he swore to your fathers, Abraham, Isaac and Jacob.'   (Deuteronomy 29:12–13)

> 'And it was not without an oath! Others became priests without any oath, but he became a priest with an oath when God said to him:

> > "The Lord has sworn
> >   and will not change his mind:
> > 'You are a priest forever.'"

> Because of this oath, Jesus has become the guarantee of a better covenant.'
>
> (Hebrews 7:20–22)

When God makes an oath, He is not appealing as we would to a higher authority; He is appealing to His own holy character. He is putting His God-ness, His deity, His character, His holiness on the line, as a guarantee of His faithfulness to His promises.

> *'When God made his promise to Abraham, since there was no-one greater for him to swear by, he swore by himself, saying, "I will surely bless you and give you many descendants."'*   (Hebrews 6:13–14)

A sacrifice

Lastly, a sacrifice seals the covenant. This is probably the most solemn and striking aspect of the three. Covenant is entered into/sealed by a sacrifice, the shedding of blood.

> *'When Moses had proclaimed every commandment of the law to all the people, he took the blood of calves, together with water, scarlet wool and branches of hyssop, and sprinkled the scroll and all the people. He said, "This is the blood of the covenant, which God has commanded you to keep."'*   (Hebrews 9:19–20)

In the covenants between God and man, the restoration of the relationship is only possible if sin is dealt with. In the Scriptures this is called 'atonement'. By it, sin is covered by something that robs it of its power to separate man from God. In the Old Testament, it was the blood of an unblemished lamb, sacrificed on the Day of Atonement, and in the New Testament, Christ fulfilled this once and for all through His death on the cross.

> *'Then he took the cup, gave thanks and offered it to them, saying, "Drink from it, all of you. This is my blood of the covenant, which is poured out for many for the forgiveness of sins."'*   (Matthew 26:27–28)

Here we see that covenant and forgiveness are linked: forgiveness is possible only through atonement, atonement is only possible through sacrifice and sacrifice means the shedding of blood.

> *'... without the shedding of blood there is no forgiveness.'*
>
> (Hebrews 9:22)

The New Covenant

The New Covenant was foretold by the prophets and was eventually fulfilled through the death and resurrection of Jesus Christ. Today, we Jews and Gentiles are together called to be the Israel of God, His covenant people – *'a chosen people, a royal priesthood, a holy nation, a people belonging to God . . . '* (1 Peter 2:9). And as individuals we can like David, become God's intimate friends:

> *'You are my friends if you do what I command. I no longer call you servants . . . I have called you friends, for everything that I learned from my Father I have made known to you.'*   (John 15:14–15)

This is the final covenant between God and man, because this one leads on to the finally perfected restoration of relationships in the New Jerusalem.

Even after the covenant with David (Psalm 89:26–29, 33–35), there were certain critical issues that stood in the way of God achieving His desire for an everlasting personal relationship with man. There was a need for a final solution to the sin problem; the law of God could show man what he should do, but it could not enable him to do it; man lacked the power to obey the law, and the motivation or desire to obey it; this produced an enormous gulf between man and God.

It is in this context that the prophets began to speak about a new covenant – not new in the sense that it totally replaced what had gone before, but new in the sense that it represented a radical breakthrough that would finally achieve the purpose of the covenants, in a new way.

' "*The time is coming,*" *declares the* LORD,
   "*when I will make a new covenant*
with the house of Israel
   and with the house of Judah.
It will not be like the covenant
   I made with their forefathers
when I took them by the hand
   to lead them out of Egypt,
because they broke my covenant,
   though I was a husband to them,"
          declares the LORD.
"*This is the covenant that I will make with the*
       house of Israel
   after that time," *declares the* LORD.
"*I will put my law in their minds*
   and write it on their hearts.
I will be their God,
   and they will be my people.
No longer will a man teach his neighbour,
   or a man his brother, saying, 'Know the LORD',
because they will all know me,
   from the least of them to the greatest,"
          declares the LORD.
"*For I will forgive their wickedness*
   and will remember their sins no more." '

(Jeremiah 31:31–34)

'*I will sprinkle clean water on you, and you will be clean; I will cleanse
you from all your impurities and from all your idols. I will give you a
new heart and put a new spirit in you; I will remove from you your heart
of stone and give you a heart of flesh. And I will put my Spirit in you and
move you to follow my decrees and be careful to keep my laws. You will
live in the land I gave your forefathers; you will be my people, and I
will be your God.*'

(Ezekiel 36:25–28)

Jesus – the final solution!

Yes! Jesus is the fulfilment of God's plan of salvation. He is the fulfilment of the 'types' in the Old Testament – the temple, the offerings, the priesthood – as we see in the following points:

1. If we are to escape judgement, we need a sin-bearer on our behalf, who has to be sinless, just as the lamb for the burnt offering on the Day of Atonement had to be without blemish.
2. In Jesus Christ, God reaches across the divide between the infinite God and finite man.

    > 'God made him who had no sin to be sin for us, so that in him we might become the righteousness of God.'   (2 Corinthians 5:21)

3. In the Incarnation, Jesus became our substitute and our representative.

    > 'For Christ died for sins once for all, the righteous for the unrighteous, to bring you to God.'   (1 Peter 3:18)

    And also,

    > 'For Christ's love compels us, because we are convinced that one died for all, and therefore all died. And he died for all, that those who live should no longer live for themselves but for him who died for them and was raised again.'   (2 Corinthians 5:14–15)

4. On the cross, Christ bore God's judgement for sin.
5. Now God can justly forgive us as we through repentance and faith, become identified with Christ's substitutionary and representative death on our behalf.

The problem of sin had been dealt with – through **covenant**!

In finishing, it became increasingly clear to me that, without exaggeration, this is one of the most powerful truths communicated by God to us. It could also be said that because of this, there is nothing that Satan hates more. If I was Satan and I wanted to get my own back at God I would seek to undermine, twist, and distort the things that are closest to God's heart. It should, therefore, not surprise us that anything with God and covenant attached to it will be at the top of Satan's hit list: Israel, the Church, marriage.

CHAPTER 4

A Spiritual Battle

What a drink!

It is now time to move on to our next stop-over and erect another pillar of stones. This has become one of the hardest chapters in this book to write. Its title aptly speaks for itself, and is undoubtedly connected to the struggle it has been to write it.

If there was ever one scripture passage that sums up for me the spiritual battle we are in, it has to be Ephesians 4:26–27:

> ' "In your anger do not sin": Do not let the sun go down while you are still angry, and do not give the devil a foothold.'

What a wonderful scripture for married couples! Paul of course did not write it for married couples, but the truths contained in this verse are most certainly applicable to husbands and wives and their need to periodically have a 'pillow conference', clearing the air of anything that has come between them during the day! It is so much broader than that, but the reality is that every breakdown in relationships can be traced back to a time when something went wrong in either word or action, and it was not sorted out. Paul is telling us that that is all it takes for us to give Satan a legal foothold in our relationships. Someone once said that sin is not the issue, as

Christ has more than adequately dealt with sin on the cross. The problem lies with unforgiven sin – this is what gives the devil such a foothold in our lives.

This applies not only to the individual but also to the corporate. This principle also holds for the local and the national Church, government, etc. John Dawson in his book *Taking Your Cities for God*, puts it this way:

> 'The only authority Satan has is a stolen human authority. He initially gains this authority when, at some point in history, human beings believe his lie, receive his accusation and are seduced into an allegiance to his plan ... Whole countries are kept in darkness by satanic lies that have become cornerstones of a particular culture.'   (p. 53)

Even though the Hebrew worldview does not recognise dualism, there is a sense in which we as human beings, over and above the rest of creation, are primarily spiritual and created to have a spiritual relationship with God. We are in a human body and encounter this world with our minds and our five physical senses. The whole of the Bible from Genesis to Revelation confirms this. It also speaks of a battle that has been going on ever since Satan was thrown out of God's presence – a battle against God waged by Satan. He is anti-God, anti-God's plan for the world and anti-God's people. He wants to distort the redemptive plans of God for us. He wants to keep people from not only having a right relationship with God but also from being His instruments and channels of healing and grace to those around us who may not yet know Him. It is a battle that is instigated in the heavenlies and worked out on the earth among people, authority figures and governmental structures. The significance of that, in the light of writing this book, I have already mentioned at the end of Chapter 3. If Satan wants to 'get at' God, there is no better way to do so than to attack that which is most precious to Him – covenant. Anything with the hand of God and covenant attached to it – whether it is the

Church, Israel or marriage – is on the top of Satan's hit-list. I am sure Paul understood this continual warfare when he wrote:

> 'For our struggle is not against flesh and blood, but against the rulers, against the authorities, against the powers of this dark world and against the spiritual forces of evil in the heavenly realms.' (Ephesians 6:12)

To continue! I take another quote from John Dawson:

> 'The city is a cluster of overlapping institutions. All institutions have a servant function. They must provide some form of service to survive. The army, the school, the hospital, the national government and the city all represent the division of labour at a corporate level. Satan seeks to rule by influencing these institutions, especially through the church, arts and entertainment and commerce. He seeks ... to make them into an extension of his kingdom.' (p. 30)

So, if the policy makers who are in charge of the political system in a country are not under the control of Christ's Spirit, then they can develop unchristian policies, which influence the minds and the actions of those under their influence. We saw this in the communist regimes of Eastern Europe and we see it closer to home as secular humanism, moral relativism and syncretism constantly erode our spiritual values.

The same applies to the Church. If the Ulster Covenant was a wrong covenant in the eyes of God, then it is sin. If it is sin – and I believe it was – then it gives Satan a foothold in the Church, and through the Church, into the nation. It set in concrete, covenantal terms, centuries of sectarian attitudes. It was also laid into the foundations upon which the states of Northern Ireland and the Republic of Ireland were eventually to be established, giving Satan *carte blanche* into the politics and spirituality of the whole of Ireland. One must not forget that the churches involved in establishing this Covenant were and still are thirty-two county, all Ireland, churches. People in the Republic of Ireland cannot therefore just sit back and say, 'It's not our problem' – spiritually it is. The border is a poor accommodation to the way politicians dealt with the results of the two Covenants of 1912 and 1916. Spiritually we are one island.

If the past leadership of these churches led their denominations and other Christians into this sinful action, then I believe it is imperative that the current leadership humble itself and seek God in repentance, thus breaking Satan's foothold. This was the role kings like Hezekiah and Josiah played in the Old Testament. They took responsibility for the evil actions of their fathers and restored the nation to its proper covenanted relationship to God. There was no other way to break the power of Satan's legal hold over them and those under them. Ownership and repentance is the only appropriate way forward.

John Dawson continues:

> 'In any conflict for a person, a family, a church or a city, discerning the nature of the enemy's lie is half the battle. Once his deception is exposed, we can now see how to apply the specific promises in the Word of God that are the basis of our faith and authority.'
>
> (p. 74)

The South African experience

A number of years ago, I had the privilege of meeting Michael Cassidy. He was the Director of African Enterprise, one of the key reconciliation ministries in South Africa. He told me that the Dutch Reformed Church repented of its covenant theology position (mentioned in Chapter 2) that legitimised the core belief systems of the Afrikaner and the Apartheid politics there – a few years later the political system fell. Like Michael Cassidy, I firmly believe that something was released by their act, in the heavenly realms. A movement of prayer exploded into the scene; political and social change followed. Michael Cassidy told me he had no reservation in believing that this action of the Dutch Reformed Church regarding the Covenant was central to all that followed. He added, 'We had one miracle – you need three!' – meaning that here in Ireland, the Presbyterian, Methodist and Church of Ireland Churches all need to do what the Dutch Reformed Church did. To repent is a massive act of humility but it brings with it cataclysmic changes in the heavenly realms!

I believe that the right order in solving the problems in Ireland is to deal with the spiritual roots of the problem before we can make significant political and social headway. Only a radical encounter with Christ can enable us to face up to the sectarianism in our hearts and our actions against our perceived enemies. We need to entrust any judging and subduing to God. This is what He said to Israel:

> 'If my people would but listen to me,
>   if Israel would follow my ways,
> how quickly would I subdue their enemies
>   and turn my hand against their foes!'   (Psalm 81:13–14)

What I quoted above from John Dawson would speak for the biblical interpretation, which I have grown to embrace over the past twenty years – an expression that has grown out of the Renewal Movement and is embraced by many of the major intercessory prayer networks that I have been associated with. But a few years ago, it was particularly refreshing for me to be introduced to the writings of Walter Wink. He appears to be saying the same things, though using a different language, and coming from different spiritual roots.

In his book *Engaging the Powers* (Fortress Press, 1992), Walter Wink writes:

> 'The act of praying is itself one of the indispensable means by which we engage the Powers. It is, in fact, that engagement at its most fundamental level, where their secret spell over us is broken

and we are re-established in a bit more of that freedom which is our birthright and potential ... intercession is the spiritual defiance of what is, in the name of what God has promised.'

(Chapter 16, 'Prayer and the Powers', p. 297)

History belongs to the intercessor

It is a remarkable fact that history belongs to us, as intercessors – those who 'stand in the gap' between man and/or situation and God – and to also realise that the all-powerful God limits Himself to work through us. What we have come to know as spiritual warfare is inseparable from intercession. Both are for all of us. Intercession is not a gift. To treat it as such is to embrace one of the biggest lies that Satan has successfully sold to the Church. Nowhere in the Scriptures do we read that intercession is a gift. It is part of our calling as *'a royal priesthood'* (1 Peter 2:9), as we join Jesus in His, as our *'great high priest'* (Hebrews 4:14), who *'always lives to intercede for* [us]' (Hebrews 7:25). Peter was addressing Jewish Christians, who knew that Christ had fulfilled through His live and death all that the Old Testament was typifying in the temple, the sacrifices and the priestly duties regarding these. The only thing that was left of that ministry after His resurrection was the priestly ministry of 'the intercessor'. We are called to join Him in this – what an incredible privilege!

Yes! We are in such a privileged position to use the most powerful weapon of all: the power to counteract what Satan is wanting to do, and the power to bring into being the purposes of God. This is a spiritual power, spiritually discerned and spiritually exercised. Through it we can actually believe the future into being. Wink says:

'If the future is thus opened, then we are no longer dealing with the unchanging, immutable God of Stoic metaphysics. Before that unchangeable God, whose whole will was fixed from all eternity, intercession is ridiculous. There is no place for intercession with a

God whose will is incapable of change. What Christians have too long worshipped is the God of Stoicism, to whose immutable will we can only surrender ourselves, conforming our wills to the unchangeable will of deity.'

(*Engaging the Powers*, ch. 16, 'Prayer and the Powers', p. 301)

Intercession changes the world and also changes what is possible to God.

Wink also describes intercessory prayer as 'impertinent, persistent, shameless, indecorous ... more like haggling in an oriental bazaar than the polite monologues of the churches. For example, Abraham with God over Sodom (Genesis 18).'

We see this intercessory role played out in people like Jeremiah, who writes:

> 'This is what the LORD says: Stand in the courtyard of the LORD's house and speak to all the people of the towns of Judah who come to worship in the house of the LORD. Tell them everything I command you; do not omit a word. Perhaps they will listen and each will turn from his evil way. Then I will relent and not bring on them the disaster I was planning because of the evil they have done.'   (Jeremiah 26:2–3)

He is fulfilling the dual role of an intercessor, as one who stands before God on behalf of men – 'everything I command you' – and then stands before men on behalf of God – 'tell them ... do not omit a word'.

We also see it in Jesus' parables about 'the persistent widow' and 'the friend who came at midnight'. Both are clear examples of how we are to be persistent in hammering away in prayer until a breakthrough comes (Luke 18:1–8; 11:5–13). Martin Luther understood this aspect of prayer well, when he said: 'Our Lord God could not but hear me; I threw the sack down before the door. I rubbed God's ear with all his promises about hearing prayer.'

I am told that when one tries to use a sledgehammer to break a hole through a concrete wall, nothing initially appears to be happening. It takes some time before the structure begins to crumble. This is because the effects of the early blows are hidden, changing the molecular structure within the wall. The wall crumbles from within, out. Persistence has its eventual and inevitable reward!

Another example is the Lord's Prayer which was originally so different from what it has become – a liturgical prayer that is rapidly recited, without a lot of thought given to its incredible content, with its powerful intercessory elements. Jesus is calling us to call unto God, as Father: '**Your Kingdom come, Your will be done, in Ireland, as it is in heaven!**'

To quote Walter Wink again:

> '... the phrases of the Lord's Prayer are not indicative but imperative – we are ordering God to bring the Kingdom near. It will not do to implore. We must command. We have been commanded to command. We are required by God to haggle with God for the sake of the sick, the obsessed, the weak, and to conform our lives to our intercessions ... History belongs to the intercessors who believe the future into being. If this is so, then intercession, far from being an escape from action, is a means of focusing for action and of creating action. By means of our intercessions we veritably cast fire upon the earth and trumpet the future into being.'
>
> (*Engaging the Powers*, ch. 16, 'Prayer and the Powers', p. 303)

When we come to the place within the intercessory process that we know the mind of God for a situation, then we have received a declaration from the very throne room of heaven. To understand this brings us to a very deep place of faith, in prayer.

Intimacy is warfare

All this about our role as intercessors in creating history can appear to be rather arrogant unless we recognise that God is

Himself **the intercessor**. He is the one who in fact initiates prayer. It is His power, not ours, that reaches out to a needy world. He is always preceding us in intercession. When we turn to intercessory prayer, we need to remind ourselves that this is already step number two in a process, and that we are joining in with God in a prayer that is already going on within us. This is something I started to become aware of shortly after I had a deeper encounter with God in the early 1970s. There were times when I was feeling, sensing a weight, a heaviness in my spirit. It was not because of anything in my own circumstances or that I was feeling depressed in my own emotions. My wife, Dorothy, would encourage me to get on my own with God in prayer; it was then that I began to realise that it was the Spirit of God within me that I was feeling. He was alerting me to intercede. As I waited on God the reason for the heaviness became apparent; scriptures and thoughts would start coming to mind, which gave me insight, understanding and articulation to the feeling.

I do not pretend to fully understand this any more than Paul did when he wrote in Romans 8:26: *'the Spirit helps us in our weakness. We do not know what we ought to pray for, but the Spirit himself intercedes for us . . . '* But a few years ago, while I was having my daily devotions, I sensed God saying to me, 'Turn to Romans 8 and embrace the groans.' In it we read about three types of groan:

1. *'The whole creation has been groaning as in the pains of childbirth'* (verse 22);
2. *'We ourselves ... groan inwardly as we wait eagerly for our adoption as sons, the redemption of our bodies'* (verse 23);
3. *'We do not know what we ought to pray for, but the Spirit himself intercedes for us* [implied in the context as 'within us'] *with groans that words cannot express'* (verse26).

Regarding intercession, the Spirit was showing me that there is a groan out there, all around us – in creation, in society – and that there is also a groan within us. We are all too aware of our own imperfections and that the imperfections in others often serve the purpose of highlighting the groan within us. God was saying to me, 'Don't run away from the groans out there, be willing to embrace them when I direct you. In this place of intercession I am looking for people who will do this. I am asking you to do it, not to overburden you, but I want you to share with My heart for this world and for the pain in others around you. This is the place of intimacy with Me, the place of sharing My heart.'

I am finding that it is then, and only then, that the third groan comes into its own. There are just simply some things we do not know how to adequately pray for. When God shares with you the pain of our young people on drugs, binge drinking, self-harming, committing suicide – how do you pray? The answer is – the Spirit of God groans within you, quite literally. You feel His pain, you carry it in your heart and you find that the Spirit is Himself interceding through you *'in accordance with God's will'* (verse 27).

There is the realisation that we don't share the deep things of our hearts with just anyone; we share them with those who are close, whom we can trust them to. God is no different. What a privilege to be called to enter into sharing the deep things of God's heart. In sharing this I am not setting myself up as some super saint. When Jesus said in John chapter 10, *'My sheep hear My voice . . . and they follow Me'* (v. 27 NASB), that included me and that included you. We can hear the voice of God both in word and in emotion, we can understand and we can respond. Walter Wink describes it as the Holy Spirit being rather like molten lava, trying to erupt to the surface from somewhere deep within us. Our response has to be one of acknowledging His presence and of allowing Him to minister in and through us in this way, 'to give articulation to the inarticulate groanings within our souls, to bring God's longings to speech.'

He goes on to say:

'For us to be open and vulnerable to both the pain of the world and the anguish of God is unendurable, unless it is matched with a precise sense of divine vocation. We must let *all* the pain picked up by our receptors pass through us. But then we must not attempt to mend it ourselves, but to do only what God calls us to do, and not one thing more ... We are not called to do everything, to heal everything, to change everything, but only to do what God asks of us. And in the asking is supplied the power to perform it ... We human beings are far too frail to bear all the pain ... We need to experience it; it is part of reality. Our task in praying is precisely that of giving speech to the Spirit's groanings within us ... We are to articulate these agonizing longings and let them pass through us to God.'

(*Engaging the Powers*, ch. 16, 'Prayer and the Powers', p. 307)

Such intercessory intimacy with God is in fact a powerful weapon in our arsenal as we warfare against Satan.

Waging spiritual warfare with the powers

As I mentioned earlier in this chapter, we have so often left out of the equation in Northern Ireland the fact that we are first of all in a spiritual battle against principalities and powers. This adds another dimension to the way we pray. Behind the socio-political forces that preside over so much of what we see around us in society, the institutions, the social structures and systems that dominate our world today, is a hidden spirituality at their centre. This has always been the case. Even in the days when Christ walked this earth 'the Roman Empire had made itself the highest value and the ultimate concern, arrogating to itself the place of God. Whether it is the Pax Romana or the Pax Britannica or the Pax Americana, empires can maintain cohesion across racial, ethnic, linguistic and national lines only by creating a bogus solidarity. This they achieve by demanding the worship of the spirituality of empire ... they did not worship the seated emperor, but only his "genius". This Latin term did not refer to his intellect but to his inspiration – the daemon, god or spirituality that animated him. His "genius" is the totality of impersonal power located in an office of surpassing might' (*Engaging the Powers*, ch. 16, 'Prayer and the Powers', p. 300).

In Daniel chapters 9 and 10 God gives us a glimpse into what is going on in the heavenly realms over a nation, as He removes the veil between the seen and the unseen worlds. The scene opens in chapter 9 with Daniel deeply mourning, with prayer and fasting, for his people. In the light of what I have mentioned above in Romans 8, he was embracing 'the groan' by choosing to face and own the sin of the nation:

> '**We** have been wicked . . . **We** have not listened to your servants the prophets . . . **We** have sinned against you . . . Therefore the curses and sworn judgments written in the Law of Moses, the servant of God, have been poured out on us, because **we** have sinned against you.'
>
> (Daniel 9:5, 6, 8, 11, emphasis added)

Unaware of what is actually going on in the unseen heavenly realms, Daniel continues to pray, finding out later that he was in contention with unseen spiritual powers. There was a very real battle going on between the angels of two kingdoms – an angel of God and a nameless Satanic prince ruling over the Persian Empire. God's angel had left His immediate presence with a message the very day Daniel had started to pray, and for the next twenty-one days the *'prince of the Persian kingdom'* actively attempted to frustrate the deliverance of that message. In chapter 10 verses 12–14 we read about the angel eventually getting through to him:

> 'Since the first day that you set your mind to gain understanding and to humble yourself before God, your words were heard, and I have come in response to them. But the prince of the Persian kingdom resisted me twenty-one days. Then Michael, one of the chief princes, came to help me, because I was detained there with the king of Persia. Now I have

come to explain to you what will happen to your people in the future, for the vision concerns a time yet to come.'

I cannot but wonder what is going on in the heavenly realms over Ireland. Is there an angel assigned by Satan over us, seeking to frustrate God's purposes here? What would have happened if Daniel had stopped praying on day twenty? Whether we like the thought of it or not, whether it fits in with our theology or not, the reality is that the principalities and powers of Satan were able to hold the purposes of God at bay! The good news is that God is more than able to overcome, and that our intercessions will ultimately prevail. A wait of twenty-one days or twenty-one years changes nothing, from a faith perspective. We cannot stop praying for what is right because our prayers are seemingly unanswered. We know from this passage, and the one in Romans 8, that not only have they been heard the very first day when we pray, but also that they were in fact initiated in our willing, available hearts, by the Spirit of God.

Our responsive prayers of intercession give God the necessary opening that enables Him to act without violating our freedom – it is a profound act of partnership. Freedom is a key word here, because the predicament we see Daniel in is derived from the fact that God does not at present effectively rule 'this world'. Satan rules it. What God is able to do in the world is hindered to a considerable degree by the rebelliousness, resistance and self-interest of the 'powers' exercising their freedom under God. God does want people to be free to become everything He created them to be, but when, for example, children's lives are stunted by sexual abuse or when one ethnic group is forced to submit to the manipulation and control of another stronger one, then what is God to do? We may pray for justice and liberation, as indeed we must, and God hears us on the very first day. But God's ability to intervene against the freedom of these rebellious people is oft times sadly restricted in ways we cannot even begin to understand. It takes considerable spiritual maturity to live in the tension between these two facts: God has heard our prayer, and the 'powers' are blocking God's response.

A clear example of this is printed into my memory. A few years ago, a number of the Protestant para-military groups were feuding against each other in an area of Belfast called the Shankill Road. They were having 'turf wars' over issues such as drug trafficking and who controlled certain areas of the Shankill, which led to an escalation of violence, and a series of 'tit for tat' murders. I felt constrained to meet with a Christian leader in the area who had a profound burden for the situation and the people. He told me that he had prayed much over the preceding thirty years for the Shankill and against what Satan was doing there. In line with what I have mentioned above, I venture to suggest that perhaps he was praying the wrong prayers.

My understanding is that if the church on the Shankill Road is a sectarian church, living under the control of the demonic lie that 'Ulster is Protestant', and is also under the stronghold of the Ulster Covenant (which the majority of their forefathers had signed), then according to the scripture at the opening of this chapter, Satan has been given a legal foothold on the Shankill Road – freedom to operate. I went on to say to him that if he could find four people in the area who were prepared to say, 'Lord, if You can further Your Kingdom purposes for Ireland through a United Ireland, I relinquish my idolatrous hold on the North to You', then he has found four people who can begin to pray against the sectarian spirit on the Shankill.

That may be a hard pill to swallow for some people, but I believe God is calling us as Christians, no matter what our traditions may be, to lay down our sectarian ways and begin to live in an opposite spirit. Whether Ireland remains divided or becomes united at some point in the future is not the issue here. What God is looking for in intercession is to find His people free from making an idol out of our national identity. We cannot pray with integrity, 'Your Kingdom come, Your will be done in Ireland as it is in heaven' if we are praying out of a sectarian spirit.

In his book *Sowing Seeds for Revival* (Sovereign World), Martin Scott writes:

> 'Jesus set us a major precedent in the Sermon on the Mount when, in using the phrase *"You have heard it said, but I say to You'*, He indicated that what is required of disciples is an inner obedience, not simply an outer conformity. In applying this principle to sins that pollute the land we will want to make sure that the sins that pollute are absent from the church, not only in an external sense, but that the very spirit behind these sins is also absent.' (p. 102)

The health of the Church is absolutely central to how we war against our enemy, Satan. We have to radically live out life as the Church in the opposite spirit to all that is an expression of the systems of this world. That is what early Christian baptism was all about; it was the outward expression of the inward reality. They had died to self and were now alive to Christ and His Kingdom reign and rule, individually and collectively as His Church. And for that, those early Christians expected to be assaulted by the powers.

I hope in concluding this chapter that your understanding of the role of the powers in blocking prayer will have expanded and will revolutionise the way we pray – I know mine has been! And that together we will be more determined to 'press on' and 'press in', as we pray for people and nations.

A final word from Walter Wink:

> 'Prayer that ignores the Powers ends up blaming God for evils committed by the Powers. Prayer that acknowledges the Powers becomes a form of social action. No struggle for justice is complete unless it has first discerned – not only the outer, political manifestations of the Powers, but also their inner spirituality – and has lifted the Powers, inner and outer, to God for transformation. Otherwise we change only the shell, and leave

the spirit intact. Prayer in the face of the Powers is a spiritual war of attrition. God's hands are effectively tied when we fail to pray. That is the dignity and urgency of our praying.'

        (*Engaging the Powers*, ch. 16, 'Prayer and the Powers', p. 317)

Let us pray . . .

CHAPTER 5

Time for Another Drink

After I received the initial picture from God about the beaver dam, I spent the next eighteen months or so researching the nature of that dam and in particular the 'covenantal' log in its foundation. In the Autumn of 1998 God turned my attention to all the water that was being held back by the dam. As a result I found myself travelling throughout 1999 to various towns and cities in Ireland (Portadown, Cork, Dublin, Limerick, Omagh, Derry, Belfast) holding a series of Prayer Days entitled '**Let the River Flow**'.

During this time, two friends of ours, Paul and Sharon Reid, wrote this song, entitled *Let Your River Flow*. It very much summed up the longing of my heart during that year and since:

> A picture of a dam
> The river could not flow
> The land was dry and tired
> The people's spirit weak.
> The logs beneath the dam
> Had been built through history
> No matter what was tried –
> the river could not flow.

> Come – O Come
> Revive this land again Lord
> Come – O Come
> And let Your river flow
> Give us a passion to see the logs removed
> And let your river flow.

My study, in preparation for this series of Prayer Days, turned out to be yet another of those landmark occasions on my journey, when God has brought me to an oasis and offered me another refreshing cool drink. I invite you sit down with me now and have one together. But first of all let me look at 'the dam' in a broader context than the Ulster Covenant one.

The dam

In the broadest sense a dam can be anything which blocks the full flow of God's Spirit in and through us – individually or corporately. It can be built into our lives through:

- Open and blatant sins such as bitterness, hatred, unforgiveness, disobedience.
- Circumstances in our lives – difficult relationships in our marriages, with family members, at church or work; unresolved conflicts from the past. These can so easily get us 'bogged down', locking us into our past.
- Contemporary/historical events. No matter how far back a negative experience has been in our personal lives or our culture, if it is still alive, it has power. In my daily devotions back then, I read 'we have all been hurt, but if you are still telling the story twenty years later, then you are not a victim of circumstances, you are a victim by choice'. While this may not be applicable to every pastoral situation, there is a core of truth in it – there comes a time when we need to make a choice to draw a line under issues, even very painful ones, if we are to move on in life.

As I have mentioned in the last chapter any of the above, if not repented of, gives Satan a legal foothold into our lives – individually or corporately (Ephesians 4:26–27).

During 1997–98 other people came to me with what they sensed were other logs in the dam – such as the Penal Laws, the potato famine, Cromwell's actions towards Ireland, Padraig Pearse's speech (Easter Rising). They all tended to have British/ Irish, Protestant/Catholic, Nationalist/Unionist components linking them. In this book I do not wish to get into dealing with any of these issues nor the multitude of other issues such as legalism, disunity, denominationalism, secular humanism, relativism, pluralism, anti-charismaticism, anti-evangelicalism and a whole lot of other anti-isms that inhibit the work of God's Spirit in and through the Church. They are for another day and for others in the Church to deal with, as the Holy Spirit directs. From my perspective of the dam in the picture – the 'log' was an integral part of the Protestant Churches' history in Ireland that God had highlighted to me specifically. One thing is sure – the dam has to go, if the river is to flow.

Looking at the 'log-jams' in our history can be very depressing stuff. Bathing in the river of God is the antidote to that.

The river

In my spirit I know that the water held back by the dam in the picture is the river of life that God wants to flow out of His Church into the nation. I acutely sense that the heart cry of God is – 'Let My river flow!'

This river flows continually through the pages of Scripture and history. It is mentioned very specifically in Ezekiel 47:1–12:

> 'The man brought me back to the entrance of the temple, and I saw water coming out from under the threshold of the temple towards the east (for the temple faced east). The water was coming down from under the south side of the temple, south of the altar. He then brought

*me out through the north gate and led me round the outside to the
outer gate facing east, and the water was flowing from the south
side.*

*As the man went eastward with a measuring line in his hand, he
measured off a thousand cubits and then led me through water that
was ankle-deep. He measured off another thousand cubits and led me
through water that was knee-deep. He measured off another thousand
and led me through water that was up to the waist. He measured off
another thousand, but now it was a river that I could not cross,
because the water had risen and was deep enough to swim in – a
river that no-one could cross. He asked me, "Son of man, do you see
this?"*

*Then he led me back to the bank of the river. When I arrived there, I
saw a great number of trees on each side of the river. He said to me,
"This water flows towards the eastern region and goes down into the
Arabah, where it enters the Sea. When it empties into the Sea, the water
there becomes fresh. Swarms of living creatures will live wherever the
river flows. There will be large numbers of fish, because this water flows
there and makes the salt water fresh; so **where the river flows
everything will live.** Fishermen will stand along the shore; from En
Gedi to En Eglaim there will be places for spreading nets. The fish will be
of many kinds – like the fish of the Great Sea. But the swamps and
marshes will not become fresh; they will be left for salt. **Fruit** trees of all
kinds will grow on both banks of the river. Their leaves will not wither,
nor will their fruit fail. Every month they will bear, because the water
from the sanctuary flows to them. Their fruit will serve for food and their
leaves for **healing**."'*   (emphasis added)

And in Revelation 22:1–2, 17:

*'Then the angel showed me the river of the water of life, as clear as
crystal, flowing from the throne of God and of the Lamb down the
middle of the main street of the city. On each side of the river stood
the tree of life, bearing twelve crops of **fruit**, yielding its fruit every
month. And the leaves of the tree are for the **healing** of the nations . . .*

The Spirit and the bride say, "Come!" And let him who hears say, "Come!" Whoever is thirsty, let him come; and whoever wishes, let him take the free gift of the water of **life.'** (emphasis added)

Other scriptures worthy of your meditation are:

'They feast in the abundance of your house;
you give them drink from your river of delights.' (Psalm 36:8)

'There is a river whose streams make glad the city of God,
the holy place where the Most High dwells.' (Psalm 46:4)

'Jesus answered her, "If you knew the gift of God and who it is that asks you for a drink, you would have asked him and he would have given you living water."' (John 4:10)

'For I will pour water on him who is thirsty,
And floods on the dry ground.' (Isaiah 44:3 NKJV)

Selwyn Hughes, interestingly, gives a definition for revival, which includes this dynamic of water and flooding. He says,

'Revival is the sudden awesome flooding of God's power upon a locality or a community of His people, stirring up the complacent, and producing the conviction and conversion of a great number of people. Revival is life at its best, life in all its fullness, life abundant, life overflowing with the grace and power of God.'

One of the key passages for me has been John 7:37–39:

'On the last and greatest day of the Feast, Jesus stood and said in a loud voice, "If anyone is thirsty, let him come to me and drink. Whoever believes in me, as the Scripture has said, streams of living water will flow from within him." By this he meant the Spirit, whom those who

*believed in him were later to receive. Up to that time the Spirit had not
been given, since Jesus had not yet been glorified.'*

'On the last and greatest day of the Feast.' This was the Feast of
Tabernacles, which was held annually and lasted for eight days,
commemorating the Israelites' journey in the wilderness, from
Egypt to Canaan. They celebrated the memory of how God
tabernacled with them in their sojourning, guiding, protecting and
providing for them with their daily supply through the manna
and quail, and even miraculously providing water on two
occasions from a rock (Numbers 20; Psalm 78:15–16). Throughout
the feast – except for the last day – they daily held a solemn
procession from the Temple to the Gihon Spring, where the priest
filled a gold pitcher with water while the choir sang Isaiah 12:3 –
'With joy you will draw water from the wells of salvation'. They then
returned to the altar where he poured out the water. This
apparently was not just an act of remembrance but it also had a
prophetic aspect to it regarding the future coming Messiah.

For me there is a real sense coming through in this passage that
day eight was actually kept for Jesus. No water was ever gathered
from Gihon, or poured out at the altar on that day – and then Jesus
stood up! You can almost here Him call out, 'I am the fulfilment of
all that you have been doing in this Feast over the centuries. I am
what you have been looking forward to, waiting for. Come to Me
and drink . . .', knowing that one day He would be smitten and
poured out for us. The apostle Paul picks up on this theme in
1 Corinthians 10:4: *'They all . . . drank the same spiritual drink; for
they drank from the spiritual rock that accompanied them, and that rock
was Christ.'* Dutch Sheets in his book *The River of God* (Regal
Books, published by Gospel Light) makes this comment on this
verse:

'This rock from which the river flowed was a type or picture of
Christ being smitten on the cross, bringing forth the water of life.
In fact, the Hebrew word for Moses striking the rock (see Exodus

17:6), and Christ being smitten (see Isaiah 53:4) are actually the same, *nakah*. When the Rock, Christ Jesus, was smitten, a river flowed to the human race.'   (p. 40)

On p. 57 of his book, Dutch Sheets also shares this insight:

> 'It was at this very feast hundreds of years earlier when Solomon's Temple was dedicated, that the priests could not stand to minister because the Temple was filled with the glory of the Lord (1 Kings 8:2–11). It was also on "the great day" of the Feast of Tabernacles that Haggai prophesied of a greater glory coming to the Temple (Haggai 2:1). " '*I will fill this house with glory*', *says the Lord of hosts. . . . 'The latter glory of this house will be greater than the former*' " (Haggai 2:7, 9).'

Surely this is reflected in the hearts of many reading this, as we yearn to see something of that Glory in His Church here in Ireland.

John Dawson, Founder of the International Reconciliation Coalition, wrote about this 'Glory' in a booklet entitled *What Christians Should Know About Reconciliation* (published by Sovereign World):

> 'Our primary objective in intercession and spiritual warfare is not the removal of the enemy but **the return of the glory** – the restoration of God's needed favour, reconciliation with God. When we encounter a spiritual stronghold, it is **not** a testimony to **the presence of a big demon, but rather to the absence of the glory**. Just as nature abhors a vacuum, so it is in the unseen realm. When the glory departs, the demons rush in. We have an enemy that swarms to open wounds and corruption – a characteristic revealed in the name, Beelzebub (Luke 11:15), which means "lord of the flies". His weapons are accusation and deception, his strongholds are places of unresolved guilt and unhealed wounds within the land.'   (emphasis added)

He goes on to say:

> 'A repentant church, confessing the sins of the nation before God
> is that nation's only hope ... The unredeemed cannot make
> atonement for the land. The pagan cannot go up into the gap and
> present the blood of the Lamb ... Our nation will be cursed,
> or blessed, according to the obedience or disobedience of the
> Church.'

To see this 'Glory' flow out of the Church into the nation is to see
this 'river' flow. That has been the increased longing in my heart
over these past eleven years. I have come to see that the 'beaver
dam' is not the issue, as John Dawson so rightly says: it is not 'the
presence of a big demon, but rather the absence of the Glory'.
What God is so much longing to see is the flowing of His river, the
river of His Spirit, and it must pain Him so much as it is His Church
that has built and continues to pursue the maintenance of the dam.

Let's have a further look at the Ezekiel 47 and Revelation 22
passages. In the first of these we read that *'where the river flows
everything will live'*. Even the Dead Sea would become fresh and
teem with fish (vv. 9–10). If God can do that to the Dead Sea then
what can He not do here in Ireland? Is there any place so spiritually
dead or barren that it cannot be transformed by the river of God?
Verse 12 adds to this by telling us that this river also brought year
long fruitfulness, and provided for healing.

The river that flowed from the threshold of the temple in
Ezekiel 47 is quite clearly the same river that is to flow from the
throne of the Lamb in Revelation 22. In the meantime, we who
are now called the temple of the Holy Spirit (1 Corinthians 3:16;
6:19) are to be the vehicles through which this same river is to
flow. There is a challenge here for us – if there are tens of
thousands of people in Ireland who profess to know Jesus as their
Saviour and Lord, then why is there not a torrent of the river of
God flowing through this island bringing life, healing and fruitfulness to the barren lives and arid places?

If this were all the revelation contained in this passage, it would be wonderful, but the reservoir runs deeper still. Jesus said, *'He who believes in Me ... From his innermost being will flow rivers of living water'* (John 7:38 NASB). 'Innermost being' is translated from the word *koilia*, which literally means 'womb'. In some versions of the Bible it is actually translated as such in Matthew 19:12, Luke 1:15 (e.g. see NASB, NKJV). Of course, a womb speaks of reproduction, of birthing of bringing forth life.

We are His birthing vessels, His incubation chambers, releasing life to those around us. Why should this surprise us? Is it not supposed to be the very life of Jesus in us that we are ministering to the world? In Galatians 4:19 we read, *'My dear children, for whom I am again in the pains of childbirth until Christ is formed in you ... '* Within the context of the preceding verses, Paul is speaking here about Christians who clearly needed to come to a new and deeper place in their relationship with Christ. He had a deep loving concern for them, he was not physically present with them, but he carried them in the womb of his heart. The King James Version speaks of him being in travail. This is a place that Christ can bring us to in intercession – a place of birthing 'God things'.

Christ is saying: 'The life in Me is to flow from you. The river in Me will flow from your womb. The things that I want to birth on earth will be carried by you, and released through you, into the earth. The harvest I am producing will be birthed from the womb of the Church.'

Two other Scriptures give us further light and understanding on this dynamic. First, Romans 8:22–27 from *The Message*:

> *'All around us we observe a pregnant creation ... it's not only around us; it's **within** us ... If we don't know how or what to pray, it doesn't matter. He does our praying in and for us, making prayer out of our wordless sighs, our aching groans. He knows us far better that we know ourselves, knows our pregnant condition, and keeps us present before God ... '*

Second, Isaiah 66:9 which asks a rhetorical question:

> ' *"Do I bring to the moment of birth*
>   *and not give delivery?" says the* Lord'.

The answer is an emphatic – No! *No! **No!***

CHAPTER 6

Legal Footholds

In this chapter I want to build on the teaching of Chapter 4 on spiritual warfare and in particular on the dynamic of giving Satan 'a legal foothold'. In his book, *The Powerhouse of God* (published by Sovereign World), Johannes Facius writes:

> 'There is one major problem that stands in the way of healing the land. That is the unconfessed historical sins of the nation. Unconfessed sin is the foothold of satanic forces, whether we speak of the individual or the nation. Unconfessed sin constitutes a basis for satanic rule. We must therefore find a way of dealing with it, if we are to see our people delivered from demonic strongholds.'

I was a few years into this journey when Dutch Sheets wrote a book entitled *Intercessory Prayer* (published by Gospel Light, Regal Books). I found his understanding invaluable regarding this whole subject of the warfare we are in. He spends a few chapters in it opening up this whole subject, taking us to a number of New Testament passages and unpacking the Greek meaning behind some key words in them.

In 2 Corinthians 4:3–4 we read:

> *'And even if our gospel is **veiled**, it is veiled to those who are perishing. The god of this age has **blinded** the minds of unbelievers, so that they cannot see the **light** of the gospel of the glory of Christ, who is the image of God.'*   (emphasis added)

The word 'veil' here, (Gk. *kalupsis*) means 'to hide, cover up, wrap around', just as bark veils the inside of a tree and our skin veils the inside of the human body. Which is just as well!

In the Greek it is interesting to observe that the word 'revelation' is *apokalupsis*: *apo* meaning – 'off or away'. A revelation is literally an unveiling, an uncovering. This is a most helpful insight regarding the process of evangelism. When we share the gospel message with people, sometimes they just don't see it. The reality is, they don't because they can't! They need to have an unveiling – a revelation. When the gospel is shared with someone, they hear it and filter it through their belief system (a veil), which can mean they hear something totally different. This is equally true of wrong mind-sets, which we hold on to as Christians.

Letting in the light

In Ephesians 1:18 Paul writes, *'I pray also that the eyes of your heart may be **enlightened** in order that you may know the hope to which he has called you...'* (emphasis added). The word 'enlighten' (Gk. *photizo*), means 'to let in the light' and is closely related to the word for light (Gk. *photismos*) meaning 'illumination'. The obvious illustration of this is the camera. When we take a photograph, the shutter opens, letting in light, bringing an image to the film. If the camera shutter does not open, there will be no image captured there. The same is true of the human soul – it makes no difference how glorious Jesus is, or how wonderful the message, if the veil (shutter) is not removed there will be no true image of Christ made in us.

Dutch Sheets also notes that the word 'repentance' does not mean (as we so often think) to 'turn and go another way, to change direction'. Such a definition matches the Greek word *epistrepho* which means 'converted', which is in fact the result of repentance. Repentance (Gk. *metanoia*) means to have 'a new knowledge or understanding', 'a change of mind'. Light has been let in, revelation has come!

This is what Paul is saying in Acts 26:17–18, in his defence before Agrippa: *'I am sending you to them* [the Gentiles] *to open their eyes and turn them from darkness to light . . .'* He was called 'to open their eyes' – to enable them to experience enlightenment, an unveiling, revelation, repentance – 'so that they may turn [*epistrepho*] from darkness to light'.

Blinded by pride

In 2 Corinthians 4:4 Paul continues to develop his thinking on being veiled. He tells us that *'The god of this age has **blinded** the minds of unbelievers . . .'* The Greek word for 'blinded' is *tuphloo*, which means 'to dull the intellect; to make blind'. It comes from the root word *tupho*, which has the meaning 'of making smoke'. So the blindness in this passage is like a smoke screen that clouds or darkens the air, impairing a person's sight, just like the difficulty a person has in a smoke filled room of even finding the door.

From this same root comes the word *tuphoo*. It is used for being high-minded, proud or inflated with self-conceit. So, we can see, there is a connection between the words 'blindness' and 'pride'. It was, after all, the sin of pride that brought about Satan's expulsion from the immediate presence of God, which he passed on to us in the Garden, and continues to use as he seeks to keep us blind.

When people choose to reject Christ, it is often based on the simple fact that they don't want to give the lordship of their lives to Him – this is pride. It is the ultimate enemy of Christ and will ultimately be dealt with when every knee bows and every tongue confesses that Christ is Lord.

Someone recently sent me a video clip of a Captain of a Naval Destroyer. One dark night he saw faint lights in the distance. He told his signalman to send a message: 'Change your course 10 degrees south.' Immediately he received the response: 'Change your direction 10 degrees north.' The proud Captain was angry that he was being challenged, so he sent a further message: 'Change your course 10 degrees south. This is the captain speaking!'

He received the response: 'Change your direction 10 degrees north. I'm Seaman Third Class Jones.' The Captain, thinking he would terrify this insubordinate sailor, wired a third message: 'Change your direction 10 degrees south. I am a battleship.' The final reply came: 'Change your course 10 degrees north. I am a lighthouse.'

This understanding of the blinding ability of pride and the other dynamics mentioned in this chapter is a tremendous clue as to how to pray for the lost or those locked into other strongholds. It was most certainly a key for me. For approximately four years I had been sharing my picture of the Beaver Dam, and what I sensed God was saying to me regarding the need for the three main Protestant Churches to repent for the Ulster Covenant, but with only minimal success.

Up to that time the majority of clergy I talked to were not able to understand or grasp the dynamic. I was finding out that many of them appeared to be, albeit unconsciously, under the control of the Ulster Covenant stronghold themselves. They were unable to either understand or respond positively to what I was sharing with them. As I have already mentioned, when we are under the influence of a stronghold, it is not a matter of not being able to see, we can't see! Just as a non-Christian is unable to understand and respond to the gospel, because a spiritual blindfold is in place (2 Corinthians 4:4), they likewise were blinded and couldn't see! You can try and argue and persuade until you are blue in the face with such a person, but nothing will change. Revelation is needed! But more about that in the next chapter.

Strongholds

Dutch Sheets then makes a connection between those verses in 2 Corinthians 4 and those in 2 Corinthians 10:3–5, where we read:

> 'For though we live in the world, we do not wage war as the world does. The weapons we fight with are not the weapons of this world. On the contrary, they have divine power to demolish **strongholds**. We **demolish arguments** and **every pretension** that sets itself up against the knowledge of God, and we take **captive every thought** to make it obedient to Christ.' (emphasis added)

What is a stronghold? The word in Greek is *ochuroma* which comes from a root word *echo*, meaning 'to have or hold'. 'Stronghold' in the New International Version, is translated in the New American Standard Bible as 'a fortress' and can also be described as a fort, a castle or a prison. Literally, it is a place in which to hold something strongly. Relating this to Satan, it implies that he has found a place within a person, something like a sinful habit or an addiction, which he can use to hold onto them strongly. When we read these verses most of us have probably interpreted this as something we do for ourselves – we demolish arguments, we take every thought captive. While this can be so, the context is certainly that of **spiritual warfare for others**.

The Living Bible makes this a lot clearer:

> 'It is true that I am an ordinary weak human being, but I don't use human plans and methods to win my battles. **I use God's mighty weapons**, not those made by men, to knock down the devil's strongholds. These weapons can break down every proud argument against God and every wall that can be built to keep men from finding him. With these weapons **I can capture rebels** and bring them back to God, and change them into men whose hearts' desire is obedience to Christ.' (emphasis added)

He is implying that there is a battle going on, and that it is primarily a spiritual battle in the heavenly realms, and then that it is secondarily worked out on the earth, in people. He is also implying that if something is broken in the heavenlies through intercessory prayer, then that 'breaking' will manifest itself on the earth. Why else would we pray for loved ones to come to faith or for prodigals to return? When we get answers to our prayers for people in a wonderful and powerful way, in essence this is what has been happening! If this is true for individual people then surely the principles that Dutch is sharing can also be applied to the corporate, to strongholds held collectively by many people within a nation.

One example of this is printed indelibly in my mind. It is related to the Drumcree parade issue. This parade is not new to people in Northern Ireland, but to put it in context for everyone else, here is a bit of the history surrounding it, written by the BBC Northern Ireland reporter Mervyn Jess:

'In 1795, the Orange Order was formed in Dan Winter's cottage in Loughgall, just a few miles from Portadown. A combination of history, tradition and to an extent a personal belief that they are in the vanguard of defending the Protestant faith, sets Portadown Orangemen apart from other members of the Order.

Changes in demography
A hundred years ago, when the lodges paraded back from Drumcree Church to their Orange Hall in the centre of Portadown, the contested Garvaghy Road section of the route was little more than a country lane.

In the late 60s and early 70s the Ballyoran housing estate was built along the route and a population of approximately 6,000 people, most of whom are Catholics, lives there today. With the changes in demography and the start of the peace process, came changes in the political climate. When parades became an issue, nationalist and Catholic residents' groups sprang up in various parts of Northern Ireland. Organised opposition to traditional "Protestant" parades through what were now mainly Catholic areas had begun.

Wider impact

Despite the history of confrontation in the Portadown area, the knock-on effect elsewhere has only been felt in more recent years. Mass protests have been staged at Drumcree when the Orange parade has been re-routed away from the Garvaghy Road, although in recent years the numbers have gone down.

Elsewhere in Northern Ireland property has been attacked and destroyed by rioters. At the height of that violence, illegal road-blocks were thrown up in a co-ordinated campaign by loyalist supporters of the Drumcree Orangemen, bringing parts of Northern Ireland to a standstill.

When the Orange parade has been forced down the Garvaghy Road amidst a massive security operation, against the wishes of the people who live there, serious disturbances have ensued in republican and nationalist areas. This year the Parades Commission has again re-routed the Orange march away from the nationalist area. The last time Orangemen paraded along the Garvaghy Road was in 1997.

This Sunday, the Portadown Lodges will continue the "trad-ition" of leaving Drumcree church, marching a few hundred yards down the hill before being brought to a halt by the police and army barrier blocking their route.'

(BBC News 4th July 2002;
http://news.bbc.co.uk/1/hi/uk/2092771.stm)

With that backdrop in mind I share the following. Mervyn Jess mentioned that the last parade down Garvaghy Road was in 1997. The following year's ban produced a massive 'stand-off', lasting several days, between the Orangemen and their supporters against the police and the British army. A very ugly scene was developing. Civil unrest was spreading throughout Northern Ireland. On the

11th of July the pressure cooker atmosphere needed to be eased, as the major day of Orange parades was the following day. It was to take the burning to death of three young boys (aged 8–10) of the Quinn family, when their house was petrol bombed, to shock at least some to come to their senses.

In January 1999, during a Prayer Gathering at the Renewal Centre, we had the sense that God wanted to call a 'solemn assembly'. The key scripture was Joel 2:12–17. Not long after that, a prayer partner in the USA wrote and shared something similar with us. And then a few months later a church in England had clearly felt that God wanted them to come to the field at Drumcree, to set up a tent and pray and fast for the week preceding the next parade on Sunday the 4th of July. They also sensed that the last day should finish with a 'solemn assembly'.

And so, on the 3rd of July, we met in a tent at Drumcree – a group from the church in England, members of the inter-church prayer group in Portadown, other leaders and praying people from across Ireland. What a scene! There was a heavy military presence as they were preparing for the worst – soldiers putting up rows of razor wire, others ploughing up the bottom of the field and turning it into a quagmire, helicopters circling overhead. Inside the tent we laid down our agendas for the day, along with the British and Irish flags at the foot of a cross. And then we worshipped. Flowing out of that time of worship came a time of deep repentance. I don't think I have ever been at a gathering where we experienced such a 'spirit of repentance'. And then it was over, a deep sense of peace settled on us and, in keeping with the wishes of the military, we packed up and went home.

The following day the Orangemen paraded to Church, the military and police were on high alert, the crowds had gathered and the world's media looked on. With the service over, the Orangemen lined up, paraded to the security cordon, handed in a letter of protest and then turned around and marched off: the crowd dissipated with them.

Mervyn Jess reported, 'in recent years the numbers have gone down'. The media don't understand why. But I do, along with everyone else gathered in that tent that day. That day, as we met there in obedience to God to hold a 'solemn assembly', He showed up and something dynamic happened in the heavenly realms over Northern Ireland in general and Drumcree specifically. A stronghold of Satan was broken.

Every time I recount that encounter with God, I am reminded of what Dutch Sheets wrote:

> 'We have weapons that are "divinely powerful" to pull down strongholds, if we would only realise it. The word "powerful" (Gk. *dunatos*), is one of the New Testament words for "miracle", and can also translated "possible". If we are facing something that seems impossible, it will take a miracle to change it. *Dunatos* is of course the word from which we get our word – "dynamite".'
>
> (p. 169)

Dynamite for the 'destruction of fortresses, 'the pulling down of strongholds'. I have been told that dynamite is often used in places like Canada to destroy beaver dams!

Dutch also points out that the Greek word for 'destruction' and 'pull down' (*kathairesis*) also has other pertinent meanings – 'to bring down with violence or demolish something'; 'to remove from office' – suggesting a new Lordship, a different ruler!

We need to remind ourselves of these things more often. And also that Christ was sent *'to proclaim freedom for the prisoners'* (Luke 4:18), and that we, the Church, have been commissioned to carry on this ministry. This is what Paul was instructing the church at Corinth to do. He not only tells them, but also us, that we have divinely empowered weapons that can demolish strongholds.

In 2 Corinthians 10, verse 5, he goes on to highlight various aspects of strongholds, which we need to understand if we are going to successfully come against them. I want to mention two key aspects here. The first of these is **'arguments'** (Gk. *logismos*).

They are the sum total of the accumulated wisdom and information learned over time. It becomes what we really believe –
our mind-set, our worldview. Interestingly, James tells us, *'Such
"wisdom" does not come from heaven, but is earthly, unspiritual, of the
devil'* (James 3:15). These *logismos* would include philosophies,
religions, racism, intellectualism, materialism, roots of rejection –
anything that causes us to think, act or react in a certain way. So if
you grow up being told that 'You are useless, stupid, fit-for-
nothing', or 'Home Rule is Rome Rule' and hearing the slogan
'For God and for Ulster', by the time you become a teenager that
is a firmly established *logismos*. It is very resistant to being told
otherwise.

The second aspect Paul mentions is '**pretensions**' (Gk. *hupsoma*),
which means 'any elevated place or lofty thing that sets itself up
against the knowledge of God'. The Living Bible calls it *'every wall
that can be built to keep men from finding him'*. Dutch connects it to
the same root of pride we discover hidden in the word 'blinded' in
2 Corinthians 4:3–4. It came to humanity at the Fall, when Adam
and Eve bought the lie *'you will be like God'* (Genesis 3:5), the
possibility of being able to be on equal footing with God Himself.
At that point we become 'not the Most High, but our own
most high – filled with pride'. So 'pretensions', 'encompass all
mind-sets that exalt themselves against the knowledge of God'.
Pride! (p. 175).

With this understanding, I will now pull up the tent pegs and
continue on with the journey. I was soon to find that the relevance
of some of this teaching was to be applied.

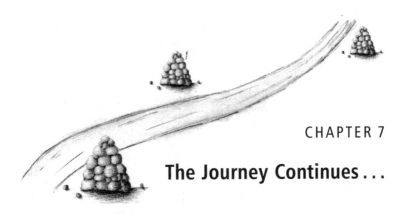

CHAPTER 7

The Journey Continues...

I now want to share with you a number of different encounters that I have had with God on this journey over the past eleven years. Each of them is a 'standing stone' for me, indelibly etched into my memory, instantly recallable, markers along the way.

A role model – Nehemiah

The process of 'birthing' mentioned at the end of the last chapter is an intercessory one. It is in the intimate place of prayer, of fellowship and communion with God, that we receive into our spirits something from the heart of God, which He wants to bring into being here on earth. One very clear example of that is found in the life of Nehemiah. His whole life, as it is recorded for us, has become a real role model for me in leadership and intercession over the past number of years.

In chapter 1 we find him in exile with some of his friends visiting him from Jerusalem. He writes:

> *'In the month of Kislev in the twentieth year, while I was in the citadel of Susa, Hanani, one of my brothers came from Judah with some other*

men, and **I questioned them about** the Jewish remnant that survived
the exile, and also **about** Jerusalem.

They said to me, "Those who survived the exile and are back in the
province are in great trouble and disgrace. The wall of Jerusalem is
broken down, and its gates have been burned with fire."

**When I heard these things, I sat down and wept. For some days I
mourned and fasted and prayed before the God of heaven.'**

(Nehemiah 1:1–4, emphasis added)

In verses 5–11 we then read Nehemiah's intercessory prayer.
Indeed, the whole chapter reveals to us the heart of a man who
was living in an intimate relationship with God. The depth of his
emotional response did not come out of a vacuum. It reveals a
man who was already close to God, who already had a heart for
his people and land.

Chapter 2 opens after a time lapse of approximately three
months. He is in the king's presence with a deep sadness of heart.
He records: 'I had not been sad in his presence before; so the king asked
me, "Why does your face look so sad when you are not ill? This can be
nothing but sadness of heart." ' To this he replied, 'Why should my
face not look sad when the city where my fathers are buried lies in ruins,
and its gates have been destroyed by fire?' When the king then asked
him, 'What is it you want?', he didn't have to say to the king, 'Do
you mind if I go off and pray about it, and then come back next
week and let you know?' We read that he immediately told the
king about wanting to return to Jerusalem to rebuild the walls, and
what he would require of the king to enable him to do that. Where
did he get all that from? I believe God gave it to him in the place of
intercession. He carried a profound burden in his heart for
months, and as he did, revelation and strategy came to him.

When you carry a general burden in your heart for Ireland, for
your local community, for the Church, do not be surprised if God
places on you a very specific one, which you are being called to
carry. And as you do, do not be surprised if God gives you further
insight and understanding regarding that burden, and how He

wants to use you to birth His Kingdom purposes regarding it. Intimacy with God is both a wonderful but also an awesomely dangerous thing! I was certainly finding it to be so!

A personal experience of travail

I now want to attempt to share with you a series of events regarding intercession that I have experienced, some of it in a very profound way. I am still quite reticent about sharing some aspects of it because it is in a way holy, sacred, to me. I do not, therefore, share it lightly.

I had been putting myself on the line before God for years in prayer for Ireland, when I had the image of the 'Beaver Dam'. Over the succeeding years I have continued to have times of heightened awareness of what God communicated to me through that picture – deeply profound feelings of heaviness and sadness in my spirit, and a rising desire to do something about it. I can certainly identify with Nehemiah in this. For me it has resulted in, as I have already mentioned, the production of a booklet – *The Ulster Covenant – revisited*; various meetings with clergy; a series of prayer gatherings throughout Ireland in 1999 on the theme of 'Let the River Flow'; my involvement in a Solemn Assembly at Drumcree 3rd July 1999; and lastly, of course, this book.

Others, including myself, have likened this intercessory process within me to the movements of a baby within the womb. That is a good analogy, as the stirrings within my spirit, like the stirrings of a developing embryo in a mother, were most certainly an assurance that it was God who had put this within me, and that it was still alive, moving progressively towards a future birthing, though I was not sure at the same time what this might actually mean or how I would experience it.

The following year I attended The British and Irish Prayer Leaders Conference 31st January – 3rd February. At the end of the morning session on 1st February, Greg Leavers, one of the Welsh conferees, came up to me and told me that he sensed God was telling him to tell me that my baby was in the breech position – he was not aware that 'pregnancy' was the analogy that I was using to carry this prayer burden. I continued on to lunch – pondering what he had said, and what it could have meant. As I sat down at the table, I was suddenly overwhelmed by deep stirrings in my spirit. Other conferees gathered round me and prayed for protection on 'the baby'. I returned to a state of peace and resumed eating my dinner. To this day I am not aware of the spiritual significance of this, or in what way the life of the 'spiritual baby' appeared to be under attack. I can only, in faith, believe that I was involved in some dimension of spiritual battle or prophetic intercession.

On a Sunday morning, approximately one month later, I was having a personal prayer time when I was again overwhelmed and moved to tears by the Spirit moving upon me. I had a very clear sense of God saying to me, 'The head is engaging.' A few days later we were hosting the Irish Prayer Leaders' Conference at the Renewal Centre. During a time of worship on the Saturday evening I was, once more, deeply stirred in my spirit, with deep weeping. There was also, quite literally, a sense of contractions, a bearing in a downward direction, deep within my pelvis – the nature of which I had never experienced before. One of the Prayer Leaders attending, herself a mother and a midwife, compared this to the contractions she experienced as her womb prepared itself for labour – known in the medical world as Brackston Hicks contractions.

The following morning, during the closing session of the Conference, the Lord spoke to us, telling us that we were on holy ground and to remove our shoes. Shortly afterwards it was felt that we, as a group, needed to prostrate ourselves before Him. During this time, I went into a full-blown birthing process of this burden I had carried. While on the floor, the Lord spoke collectively to us regarding the way His name was blasphemed throughout Ireland, and of the pain that this caused Him. He spoke also of His desire to renew us in our covenant relationship with Him as His people – the Church. As we entered into a time of repentance over this, it was felt that we could not enter into the new, without dealing with the obstacle of wrong covenants we had entered into (none of this being instigated by me!).

Prior to the Conference I had a deep sense in my spirit that during that year we needed to arrange a weekend to further pray into some of the issues surrounding the Ulster Covenant. I felt that such a weekend needed to have representatives of the different traditions in Ireland, along with Scots/Ulster Scots and English. Unknown to me, God had that combination attending the Conference. Before my very eyes, in a perfect spiritual environment, the time had come. As I mentioned, this was not instigated by me – in fact I was at this point totally incapacitated! During each phase of the group praying through this, I moved in tandem with them, to birth what I had been carrying in my spirit over the past few years.

The outcome of this time of intercession was that I came to a place of incredible inner peace and joy. That which I had been carrying in faith was birthed. At 1.25pm on Sunday 12th March 2000 – the baby was born! I have never since that day carried the issue of 'The Ulster Covenant' in the same way. It is not something I carry within me as a prayer burden, but rather more like carrying a 'baby in arms'! Obviously, there is the need to continue to pray for God's protection of this 'new baby', and in faith to be on the lookout for the earthly outworking of what God accomplished in the heavenlies that morning. One thing is certain, I rest in an incredible place of faith. It is not an issue of 'if' but rather 'when', regarding the repentance of the Ulster Covenant, the removal of the 'log jam', the flowing forth of the 'River of God' across Ireland. God recently put it in another way to me: 'When I place an intercessory burden into your spirit it is a declaration of intent from My throne room.' What a thought! What a privilege!

One clear indication that something had indeed shifted in the heavenlies came approximately six weeks after the Prayer Leaders'

Conference, as I began to notice, on sharing about the Ulster Covenant with people, and with clergy in particular, that they were beginning to understand what I was talking about. The veil was being removed!

IHOP

IHOP – for any Americans reading this – does not only mean the International House of Pancakes! In the autumn of that year, my wife Dorothy and I went to Kansas, Missouri, to attend a Harp and Bowl Conference, organised by the International House of Prayer (IHOP). That same year, the founders of the Christian Renewal Centre, the Rev. Cecil and Myrtle Kerr, had just retired and we were in the process of transitioning to become a House of Prayer for Ireland – something which God had put on my heart, back in 1979, when he called my wife Dorothy and me to leave secular employment and go into 'full-time' ministry. The same foundations of reconciliation and renewal still remained, but we realised the need to futurise the ministry.[1] A ministry, which was born out of a move of the Spirit in Ireland, was now becoming a ministry that was praying for a new move of the Spirit, especially in the Church, and among the youth and young adults of Ireland.

Part of our time in Kansas was spent with two of the leadership team at IHOP – Dwayne Roberts and Kirk Bennett – as we were eager to find out all we could about the ever growing phenomena around the world of 'Houses of Prayer'. During one of the sessions with us, one of them suddenly stopped and asked the question, without any prior knowledge of my experience earlier that year, 'Did you birth something?' He then went on to share how God had shown him a baby that had just been born and like, Moses, it was hidden in the bulrushes for protection. He then spoke words similar to these to me: 'That which has been born in prayer will be raised up to become the deliverer of that which it was born to deliver.' I may not have felt that I needed that sort of confirmation from God, but He must have known I did. It was certainly a powerful endorsement from Him, that this journey of prayer that I was on was His idea and not mine!

Another picture!

In June 1998, the new legislative Assembly for Northern Ireland was formed after a Referendum a few weeks earlier. Everyone was anticipating some sort of breakthrough in the political stalemate of those days. The Assembly had been going for a few weeks, when I woke in the middle of the night with my second powerful image/vision/dream. I saw people trying to bring together the positive poles of two powerful magnets. They came very close to connecting them, when they repelled each other. This repeated itself a few times and every time they again repelled each other. I then had a sense that God was saying to me that gathered around the table in the new Assembly were two groups of people who were covenanted against each other. Like the two magnets, they were destined to repel each other, and no matter how many times the British and Irish Governments tried to bring them together, their efforts would fail. Built into the Assembly was the mechanism for its own downfall. It took two encounters with people from outside Ireland to concretise what God was saying to me here. I will share with you shortly my meetings with them.

The suspension of the Assembly on the 14th October 2002, bringing Northern Ireland once again under direct rule from Westminster, was therefore no surprise to me. Neither were the recent attempts of getting devolved government going again in the last elections in November 2003. What we have ended up with is an unworkable bi-party state, with Ian Paisley's Democratic Unionist Party at one extreme and Gerry Adam's Sinn Fein at the other. They are positionally the epitome of the Covenants of 1912 and 1916. Both are looking for totally opposite outcomes from the political process: one, the maintenance of the union with Britain, the other a United Ireland. Both have been underscored with the spiritual power of covenant.

What this is confirming to me is that we are trying to deal with what is primarily a spiritual problem, by political and social means. We are therefore treating 'fruits' rather than 'roots'. That is why I have felt that the title of this book should be *Heal Not Lightly*, coming from Jeremiah 8:11:

> 'They have healed the wound of my people lightly,
>   saying, "Peace, peace,"
>   when there is no peace.'
>
> (RSV)

Until we realise that we are dealing with something with spiritual roots, nothing is going to radically change. Many are talking of political stalemate and of our 'digging a deeper hole for ourselves'. This is a time of wonderful opportunity for the Church in Ireland, and especially for its leadership, to rise up and give a lead – not a political lead, but to exercise their authority in the spiritual realm, in giving a lead through humility and repentance. As I have already mentioned elsewhere in this book, changes in the heavenly realms will ultimately manifest themselves in the social and political realms.

We need to realise afresh that the primary authority in the nation is not the secular one but the Church. It is the Church that should be determining what happens in the nation as we exercise our authority in the heavenly realms against Satan's principalities and powers (Ephesians 6:12). I believe this authority is maximised when the spiritual leadership stands together in unity. They act in a sense like an umbrella. If there are holes in it, the people underneath will get wet. In a day when great forward strides have been made in the issue of Church unity, unresolved issues such as the Ulster Covenant one, stand as a barrier to furthering this in a deeper, more significant way. It is a shallow unity if we cannot recognise the wrongs of the past – mentioned in Chapters 2 and 3 – and say sorry.

The other magnet!

There was a point in time, in my research of the Ulster Covenant, when I became aware of questions within me regarding the role of Padraig Pearse in all of this. I then remembered a small booklet I had, called *Ireland: the Blood Sacrifice*, co-written by Paddy Monaghan and Eugene Boyle in 1986. In it they wrote about the birth of the Irish Republic and of the happenings on Easter Sunday 1912 – The Easter Rising:

' . . . a small group of revolutionaries took over the centre of Dublin city and held it for a week until it was reduced to rubble by the artillery of the British Army. The leaders, all signatories to the Proclamation of the Irish Republic, were executed. This event, solemnly commemorated every Easter, has become the foundation story of the Irish Republic. It differs in one regard from most other foundation stories. It is a religious as well as a political event. According to the Commandant-General of the rebels, they were laying down their lives for Ireland as Christ laid down his life for the world; they were redeeming Ireland with their blood. And they succeeded. A whole new generation of revolutionaries sprang up after them as Pearse, the Commandant-General, had predicted.

They took up the War of Independence, as it has come to be known, and won the measure of political freedom Ireland enjoys today. Idealistic young people rallied to the call and gave their lives as Christ and Pearse had done and still do, for there is a measure of freedom still to be won. There is still the North . . . It is our contention that what Pearse did, what the revolutionaries of 1916 did, was based on a premise entirely opposite to the sacrifice of Christ – the unconscious re-enactment of an ancient pagan myth, a blood sacrifice to an earth goddess. To explain this we have to go back in history.

Ancient Celtic Mythology

Before Christianity came to Ireland in the 5th century, our pagan ancestors used to worship many gods, one of whom was the earth goddess called "Eire", who was regarded as the bride of a king who "married" her at Tara at his inauguration. From the earliest times Ireland was thought of as a woman and this image continues vividly and powerfully to the present day. Some early writings on this period record that though Eire, symbolising the land, was old and ugly, when a human sacrifice was made to her, she became young and beautiful, a fit bride for the king. Thus a young man had to be sacrificed, his blood seeping down into the earth. Even before the coming of St. Patrick this practice of human sacrifice was abolished and an animal substituted for the young man. Nevertheless the memory of the ancient myth, the withered old hag who personified the land being transformed into a beautiful young girl by the blood sacrifice of young men, remained. It has survived in the two images of Ireland with which we are still familiar, the young girl queen Caithlin Ni hUllachain or Roisin Dubh and the old woman, the Sean Bhean Bhoct, the Hag of Beara.

Revival of Celtic Myth in 19th Century

It was the poets who kept the Celtic myth alive and it is a recurring theme in their writings. They had accepted Christianity on one level but without, on another level, letting go of paganism and found no difficulty in holding two incompatible beliefs at the same time. Among the key scholars promoting this myth in the late 1880s and 1890s were poets like William Butler Yeats and George Russell. Yeats' play "Caithlin Ni hUllachain" was performed in 1902 and this myth is portrayed in it with terrifying clarity. However both of these men were heavily influenced by the occult. Yeats was a spiritualist and a member of the occult Society of the Golden Dawn, whose membership also included Maude Gonne. Yeats attempted to set up a druidic order to revive old Celtic worship and used magic; his wife was a medium. George Russell was a mystic and had visions of Celtic gods and goddesses; he was a close friend and collaborator with Yeats.

1916 Rebellion

Padhraig Pearse, a poet and school teacher, was particularly influenced by Yeats and so he came to believe that only the blood sacrifice could rejuvenate the jaded land of Ireland. In his writings, plays and speeches in the years before the 1916 Rebellion, Pearse taught that:

1. Holiness was identical with extreme nationalism: "bloodshed is a cleansing and a sanctifying thing".
2. Irish nationalism was identical with Christianity.
3. Just as Christ laid down his life for mankind so Ireland or Eire was calling on her young men to lay down their lives for her.

This was one of the reasons Pearse picked Easter Sunday for the Rebellion, so that the New Ireland he wanted would be identified with the Rising of Jesus ... It is significant that the Roman Catholic hierarchy of the time had excommunicated all members of the I.R.B. (Irish Republican Brotherhood), the secret revolutionary society that had really organised the rebellion and in which Pearse became the prime mover. Pearse saw himself as performing a supremely Christian act but his church leaders disagreed with him. They excommunicated him. They saw, however dimly, that the spirit which was driving Pearse was not the Spirit of God but the ancient spirit of Eire, still demanding the lives of her young men.'

The mix was there: deity/spirituality; land; sacrifice. This was the stuff of Covenant!

Confirmation from afar

It was around this time that I attended a European Prayer Leaders Conference in Yverdon, Switzerland. This was the first conference of this nature that I had attended since leaving our previous ministry in Holland, in 1991. Europe was no longer my primary area of ministry, but I had a strong sense that I should attend this specific one. For the first two days, I was beginning to doubt if I had heard God properly. I was asking myself, 'What on earth am I doing here?' It was great to meet old friends etc., but they were praying into issues that I found very hard to connect with.

One of the speakers, scheduled for the second half of the Conference, was John Mulinde. He leads one of Africa's key intercessory ministries – 'World Trumpet Ministries' – and grew up through the holocausts in Uganda, Rwanda and Burundi. I could hardly believe my ears, when he stood up and said that he was going to speak about covenants. As he spoke, I sat there and ticked off my list one issue after another, things, observations that I had made regarding the role of the Ulster Covenant in Ireland.

Over a cup of coffee I had the opportunity to have a chat with him about my picture of the beaver dam and where I sensed God was leading me in it all. During that conversation, he asked me a question; 'Where is the counter-covenant?' He then continued to explain his question. As he did, it was turning out to be a missing key piece of the jig-saw.

He told me that in his culture people made covenants over everything, even to bring in the harvest together. It produces a very secure basis to work on as a society. But, on the other hand, if you make a covenant against someone else, they will invariably make a covenant against you. You then end up in what has been coined 'a counter-covenantal relationship'. This can happen at an interpersonal level between two people and even at an ethnic level. He told me that this is what happened between the Hutu and the Tutsi people in Rwanda. The horrendous result was the holocaust.

A few years after that, Alistair Petrie, the researcher for Sentinel Ministries 'Transformations' videos, was to be in Belfast to launch their second video. He got in touch with me, saying that he would be in Northern Ireland for two days and could he meet me. It turned out that he had a copy of my booklet *The Ulster Covenant – revisited* and wanted to have a chat with me about it. He added a further insight, coming out of his work as a researcher.

He too talked in terms of counter-covenantal societies and put it into the context of the Northern Irish situation. His sense was that we were presently in the worst possible situation, worse than anything else in the previous thirty years of the current conflict. He explained this as follows:

1. The underdog rises up, grows in confidence in the political arena and sees the fulfilment of its covenanted ideology looming on the horizon.
2. Conversely, the other group that has been in the ascendancy begins to fragment and feels that its back is being pushed into a corner and is losing a grip on its covenanted position.
3. The stage is set for Satan to flick a switch in the corporate psyche of the second group mentioned. The possibility of holocaust becomes very real. This was his explanation of the Rwandan and the Bosnian genocides and indeed any situation where two people groups are at odds with each other and are using their national identity, their deity and land as a means to unite themselves to defend their positions. This is an extremely potent mix!

This is very sobering. Some people have said to me, 'That will never happen here.' Who says so? That is exactly what they said in Rwanda. And what of Hitler? And 1912? What would have happened if the Unionists had not got their way? Would Lord Carson have used his army? Would the quarter of one million men who signed the Ulster Covenant have stood with them in support? And what could happen if we ever get to the place when the Union with Britain is on the line? The changes in our demographics and in the last election results could be interpreted to point in that direction.

It is my sense that the major threat to peace in Northern Ireland will not come from the Nationalist community. They are feeling increasingly secure in their position, politically. They are on target regarding the fulfilment of their agenda for a United Ireland. On the other hand, it is the fragmented Unionist community that is feeling most threatened and from which any major future resistance could come.

That is all the more reason for this book, and what I believe God wants to communicate to His Church through it. There is another way! We don't have to wander around in circles and die in the spiritual wilderness that we have made through damming the flow of the river of God. We have within us, the Church, the where-withal, the capacity to see God's healing flow across this land, North and South. I will expand further on this in the remaining two chapters.

Note

1. See Appendix 3 for further information on the ministry of the Christian Renewal Centre – *a House of Prayer for Ireland* – or visit our website, www.crc-rostrevor.org

CHAPTER 8

At the River Bank

'Now then, you and all these people, get ready to cross the ... River into the land I am about to give them ... As I was with Moses, so I will be with you; I will never leave you nor forsake you. Be strong and courageous, because you will lead these people to inherit the land ... go in and take possession of the land the LORD your God is giving you for your own.' (Joshua 1:2, 5–6, 11)

God is looking for Joshua type leadership in these days, which will rise up and lead the people of God into their inheritance. Not a physical land, as He did for the Israelites, but spiritually. There is something God has given for each of us to do, to enter into, as we live for Him. I have written in the margin of my Bible beside these verses quoted above, the question: 'What is the land that God has given to me, to possess?' Where I am now, as Director of the Christian Renewal Centre, is a part of that. But collectively, what has God given to us to enter into, to inherit as the Church in Ireland? Broadly speaking, it is the Kingdom of God. What we have allowed Satan to do over the centuries has, by and large, robbed us of our full inheritance. But we can claim it back. Removing Satan's spiritual powerbases, such as the Ulster Covenant, is a part of that.

And we can start that process now! We do not have to wait for the Presbyterian Assembly, the Church of Ireland Synod or the Methodist Conference to repent. This is something that these governing bodies alone can do, but we can cut the spiritual power of the Ulster Covenant off, one by one, over our families.

In Numbers 14:18 we read:

> 'The LORD is longsuffering and abundant in mercy, forgiving iniquity and transgression; but He by no means clears the guilty, visiting **the iniquity of the fathers** on the children to the third and fourth generation.'
> (NKJV, emphasis added)

Notice what it says about the 'fathers'. Within that context, I am the third generation from the signing of the Covenant by over 90% of my grandfather's generation. While I have not been able to ascertain if my grandfather signed it or not, others have been able to find out from the Public Records Office website – www.proni.gov.uk.

Other scriptures also specifically mention the place of the 'fathers':

> 'But if they confess their iniquity and the **iniquity of their fathers**, with their unfaithfulness in which they were unfaithful to Me, and that they also have walked contrary to Me...'
> (Leviticus 26:40 NKJV, emphasis added)

> 'You show loving-kindness to thousands, and repay the **iniquity of the fathers** into the bosom of their children after them – the Great, the Mighty God, whose name is the LORD of hosts.'
> (Jeremiah 32:18 NKJV, emphasis added)

> 'Please let Your ear be attentive and Your eyes open, that You may hear the prayer of Your servant which I pray before You now, day and night, for the children of Israel Your servants, and confess the sins of the

*children of Israel which we have sinned against You. Both **my father's
house** and I have sinned.'*   (Nehemiah 1:6 NKJV, emphasis added)

*'Then those of Israelite lineage separated themselves from all foreigners;
and they stood and confessed their sins and the **iniquities of their
fathers.'***   (Nehemiah 9:2 NKJV, emphasis added)

*'O Lord, according to all Your righteousness, I pray, let Your anger
and Your fury be turned away from Your city Jerusalem, Your holy
mountain; because for our sins, and for the **iniquities of our fathers**,
Jerusalem and Your people are a reproach to all those around us.'*
                (Daniel 9:16 NKJV, emphasis added)

As I have mentioned, the Bible decrees that it is the iniquities of
the **fathers** that will be visited upon the children to the third and
fourth generation. It is of interest to note that as God was the
Father of Jesus, there was no generational sin or iniquity for Jesus
to inherit. But as the father of my household, on the basis of the
above verses, I have had to confess my sins and the sins of my
fathers regarding the Ulster Covenant and have cut off its
influence over my life and my family, and especially over my son.

Before I invite you to do likewise, I want to take a bit of time
here to develop what I understand the Scriptures teach us on this
subject of generational sin or iniquity.

Dr Bonnie Eaker Weil, a secular researcher on adultery, wrote:

'At that moment I began to see that adultery – much like
alcoholism or abuse – was a multi-generational thing ... I've
counselled more than 1,000 couples, 80 percent because one or
the other had been unfaithful. In nine out of ten cases, sometimes
involving four generations with grandparents as well as parents
and children, at least one partner was the adult child of an
adulterer.'   (*Daily Express*, 3rd August 1993)

Her conclusion – that children are affected by the behaviour of
their recent generational line – is confirmed by Christian and non-
Christian counsellors alike.

Ruth Hawkey, in her booklet *Freedom from Generational Sin* (published by New Wine Press), cites several examples from her own counselling experience. Here is one of them:

> 'As we were teaching on this subject, a man who was at the seminar suddenly realised that he, his father, his grandfather and now his sons had all been involved with molesting young boys. Surprisingly, this gave him a great deal of hope, rather than adding to his despair, for he began to see a reason for his sin and for the family weakness which was so evident within himself and his sons. He also began to see the possibility of the sin and the iniquity being dealt with at the cross.'

The Old Testament writers such as Jeremiah understood this dynamic when he wrote,

> '*Our fathers sinned and are no more,*
> *But we bear their iniquities.*'   (Lamentations 5:7 NKJV)

I want to give you three separate examples of this.

1. Abraham

This dynamic of our bearing the iniquities of our fathers is recorded very early in the Scriptures in the family line of Abraham. In Genesis 12:11–13 and 20:2, we have two accounts of Abraham, through fear, referring to his wife Sarah as his sister. His son Isaac repeats this in Genesis 26:6–7. A few chapters further on this dynamic appears again, when Jacob is deceived into marrying Leah instead of Rachel (Genesis 29:25). Jacob in turn had deceived Isaac into giving him the blessing of the firstborn, by pretending to be Esau (Genesis 27:35) and his sons deceive him into believing that Joseph was killed by a wild animal instead of being sold into slavery (Genesis 37:31–32).

Yet in all of this God declared Abraham 'not guilty'. In Romans

4:3, 9, 22; Galatians 3:6 and James 2:23, Paul and James quote Genesis 15:6, *'Abraham believed the* LORD, *and he credited it to him as righteousness.'* Nevertheless his sin/transgression issue of lying and deception was not 'cleared' by God. It was visited upon the following generations.

2. David

Another example from the Scriptures is found in the life of David and his descendants. He secretly had a sexual relationship with another man's wife – the wife of one of his most faithful and trusted mighty men, Uriah. She became pregnant and David brought her husband back from the battlefield under false pretences, in the hope that he would go home and have sexual intercourse with his wife, thus hoping to disguise the identity of the baby's real father. The whole thing back-fired on him, when Uriah didn't fully comply. David was so desperate about not being found out that he sent the husband back to the battle line, carrying a private letter to the commander telling him to ensure that Uriah was killed in battle.

David had hardened his heart against God, and it was only when fully confronted with his sin by Nathan the prophet, that David finally repented to God. When he repented, God in His great mercy forgave him and took away his sin.

> *'So David said to Nathan, "I have sinned against the* LORD.*" And Nathan said to David, "The* LORD *also has put away your sin; you shall not die."'* (2 Samuel 12:13 NKJV)

David's repentance was very real; he even wrote Psalm 51 as an expression of his heartfelt grief at the evil he had committed, and also his assurance of the relief and the release that his genuine repentance would bring. There is no question from Scripture that God did not forgive him and put away his sin. On the contrary, he is recorded as being a *'man after* [God's] *own heart'* (Acts 13:22;

cf. 1 Samuel 13:14). Yet despite the great blessings that followed his repentance, the Lord, through Nathan, outlined that his sin nevertheless had consequences. One of these was a generational curse upon his descendants,

> 'Now therefore, the sword shall never depart from your house, because you have despised Me, and have taken the wife of Uriah the Hittite to be your wife.'   (2 Samuel 12:10 NKJV)

The Scriptures clearly catalogue the outworking of this curse on David's family:

- Amnon raped his sister Tamar.
- Absalom then killed Amnon.
- Absalom tried to overthrow his father David, and in the end was killed, while humiliatingly hanging helplessly from a tree by his hair.
- Solomon had Adonijah executed.

Spiritual principles explain actions and their consequences. The consequences of David's sin were to have an immediate out-working on David's offspring. Nathan declared, 'the child also who is born to you shall surely die' (2 Samuel 12:14 NKJV). On the seventh day the child died.

David was guilty of adultery, treachery and murder. He acknowledged his sin to God and it was forgiven but not cleared as regards the iniquity being visited upon his descendants for several generations. His children did not bear his guilt, yet Scripture clearly shows they did suffer very severe consequences, resulting directly from their father's sin.

3. Manasseh

Manasseh was one of the most wicked and tyrannical kings in Scripture. 2 Kings 21:2–9 records:

'He did evil in the eyes of the LORD, *following the detestable practices of the nations the* LORD *had driven out before the Israelites. He rebuilt the high places his father Hezekiah had destroyed; he also erected altars to Baal and made an Asherah pole, as Ahab king of Israel had done. He bowed down to all the starry hosts and worshipped them. He built altars in the temple of the* LORD, *of which the* LORD *had said, "In Jerusalem I will put my Name." In both courts of the temple of the* LORD, *he built altars to all the starry hosts. He sacrificed his own son in the fire, practised sorcery and divination, and consulted mediums and spiritists. He did much evil in the eyes of the* LORD, *provoking him to anger.*

He took the carved Asherah pole he had made and put it in the temple, of which the LORD *had said to David and to his son Solomon, "In this temple and in Jerusalem, which I have chosen out of all the tribes of Israel, I will put my Name forever. I will not again make the feet of the Israelites wander from the land I gave their forefathers, if only they will be careful to do everything I commanded them and will keep the whole Law that my servant Moses gave them." But the people did not listen. Manasseh led them astray, so that they did more evil than the nations the* LORD *had destroyed before the Israelites.'*

God then goes on to declare through his prophets what the consequences of his sinful actions would be in due time.

'Manasseh king of Judah has committed these detestable sins ... therefore ... I am going to bring such disaster on Jerusalem and Judah that the ears of everyone who hears it will tingle. I will stretch out over Jerusalem the measuring line used against Samaria and the plumb-line used against the house of Ahab. I will wipe out Jerusalem as one wipes a dish, wiping it and turning it upside-down.'   (2 Kings 21:11–13)

And so it was, when a bigger tyrant, the king of Assyria defeated him, he put him in fetters and trailed him off to a Babylonian prison, where he finally turned to God in repentance. God heard his prayer and brought him back to Jerusalem, where he spent the rest of his days undoing the previous evils he had committed

(2 Chronicles 33:10–19). Yet the consequences that God attached to Manasseh's original sins continued to manifest themselves three generations later.

His son Amon undid his father's latter good works and reintroduced the former evil back into the land (2 Kings 21:19–20). However, he was followed by Manasseh's grandson Josiah, who repeated his father's latter good works and undid all the evils of Amon, working hard to restore the righteous principles of the Kingdom of God into the land (2 Kings 23). He was such a good king *'in the eyes of the LORD'* (2 Kings 22:2), that God did not bring the consequences of Manasseh's actions about until Josiah had died:

> *'Because your heart was responsive and you humbled yourself before the LORD when you heard what I have spoken against this place and against its people, that they would become accursed and laid waste, and because you tore your clothes and wept in my presence, I have heard you, declares the LORD. Therefore, I will gather you to your fathers, and you will be buried in peace. Your eyes will not see all the disaster I am going to bring on this place.'*   (2 Kings 22:19–20)

For nearly twenty years the nation had experienced revival under Josiah's rulership. Following his death the prophesied calamities were then fulfilled – religious apostasy, political and moral disintegration, culminating in the Babylonian captivity. Jeremiah was God's prophet to the nation at that time. He was called by God to tell the people the cause of the various forms of destruction they were being handed over to. Notice it was because of Manasseh's sin!

> *' "I will send four kinds of destroyers against them," declares the LORD, "the sword to kill and the dogs to drag away and the birds of the air and the beasts of the earth to devour and destroy. I will make them abhorrent to all the kingdoms of the earth because of what Manasseh son of Hezekiah king of Judah did in Jerusalem." '*   (Jeremiah 15:3–4)

Peter Wagner in his book *Praying with Power* (Regal Books, published by Gospel Light) writes on this issue of 'sin' and 'iniquity':

> '**Sin is the specific act that was committed; the iniquity refers to the state of guilt resulting from that sin** that is passed down through the generations. We Americans, for example, suffer today from the corrupting effects of the iniquity of slavery in our society although none of us alive ever personally engaged in the slave trade itself.'

He goes on to say,

> 'I believe that the phrase "third or fourth generation" can be understood as a figure of speech, meaning that it goes on and on. How long? Until the act of sin, which began the malignant process, is remitted by the shedding of blood.'

The only blood now necessary and available for remitting sins is the blood of Jesus! As Isaiah 53 says:

> '*He was wounded for our transgressions,*
> *He was bruised for our iniquities;*
> *The chastisement for our peace was upon Him,*
> *And by His stripes we are healed.*'   (Isaiah 53:5 NKJV)

His death was an all-sufficient one for us. Not only do we get our forgiveness there, but we also have One who took upon Himself the outworking of the consequences of the sin, both personal and generational.

Other more contemporary examples

Ken Symington, in his teaching notes entitled *Understanding Generational Issues* cites an example nearer to home:

'My own nation is a nation blighted by religious aggression ...
where many who claim Christ as their own have in His Name
inspired acts of terrible violence among their followers.'

He then gives several quotes from various Irish history books to
make his point:

'On the 1st of July 1795, the Rev. Mr Monsell, a Protestant
clergyman of Portadown, invited his flock to celebrate the
anniversary of the battle of the Boyne by attending church, and
he preached such a sermon against the Catholics that his
congregation fell on every Catholic they met on the way home,
beat them cruelly, and finished the day by murdering two
farmer's sons, who were quietly at work in a bog.'

(Mooney's *History of Ireland*, 1846, p. 876)

The Orange Order's history[1] itself gives more details of this
reverend gentleman from Portadown:

'Very few of the resident gentry of the Country joined us in the
first instance. Of those few were my old friend, Joseph Atkinson,
Esq., already mentioned; the Revd. George Maunsile, (sic
Maunsell) of Drumcree, afterwards Dean of Leighlin.'

(*The Formation of the Orange Order*, p. 18)

There can be little doubt that the Rev. Monsell of Portadown in
1795, described in Mooney's *History of Ireland* is the same Rev.
Maunsell who was Rector of Drumcree, Portadown, between
1781 and 1804 and one of the founding members of the Orange
Order. This could explain the spiritual roots to the 'Drumcree
crisis' (mentioned in Chapter 6), which suddenly erupted in 1995.

It was on the first Sunday in July 1995 that the Orange parade
left the Drumcree Parish church after its annual service and was
refused entrance to the nearby Catholic housing estate on the
Garvaghy Road, triggering off the now annual confrontation that

typifies the whole of the Northern Ireland problem that is several hundred years old.

That this has come to a head in Portadown exactly two hundred years to the anniversary (i.e. the first Sunday in July 1795 – first Sunday in July 1995) is unlikely to be a mere coincidence of history.

I believe that the God of Justice is doing business with the Northern Ireland Christian community – those who are 'called by His Name'. Singing 'How great Thou art', wearing a sash, has not moved God's hand, nor will it. He does business with those who are the peacemakers, with those who deal in forgiveness. The proud He opposes but draws near to those with a broken heart and a contrite spirit.

In his book referred to earlier, Peter Wagner gives us a powerful up-to-date illustration of this regarding two First Nation tribes in Southern California – the Pachangas and the Sobobas. Before the arrival of the Europeans they had become bitter enemies. On one occasion the Pachangas invaded the territory of the Sobobas and the warriors of both tribes ended up locked in a fierce battle. As the struggle went on, the Soboba women and children escaped and hid themselves from danger, deep in a canyon of the San Jacinto Mountains. When the Pachanga warriors overcame the Sobobas they followed the trail of the women and children into the canyon, where they slaughtered every one of them in cold blood. To this day that place is called 'Massacre Canyon'.

This massacre became a stronghold for the devil. As the generations went by, the Sobobas as a group degenerated and became miserable. Destruction and death increased to such a level that it became officially known as the most violent Indian reservation in the United States – averaging a murder a month, Indian killing Indian.

Meanwhile the whites settled in Hemet and it became a flourishing retirement community. In one of the churches there, during a conference, some white people repented of their ancestral sins against the Indians, with deep reconciliation following. As a result a number of Sobobas and Pachangas became Christians and they began to grow in their faith.

Some time later it was felt that more should be done about the issue, so they met in Massacre Canyon where the shedding of innocent Soboba blood had taken place. As they stood on that defiled land, they spent some time worshipping and exalting Jesus Christ as the rightful Lord of Massacre Canyon and of the Soboba Nation. They then went into an extended time of prayer, asking God to cleanse the land they were standing on of the bloodguilt of past generations.

At one point a Christian Pachanga publicly addressed a Christian Soboba, confessing the sins of the ancestors and asking forgiveness for the massacre. Not a dry eye could be seen in the canyon when the Soboba responded, sincerely forgiving the Pachanga.

Together the group asked God to forgive the sin of the massacre, and then thanked Him for remitting the sin on the basis of the blood shed by Jesus Christ. To commemorate Jesus' death they all took Holy Communion, proclaiming the power of the blood of Christ to be greater than the evil power that was released when innocent blood was shed there.

Peter Wagner was recounting that incident four years after it took place. Up to that time, not a single murder had been committed on the Soboba Reservation, except for one totally unrelated case.

Looking further at God's provision within the New Covenant

For some people the question is – doesn't the miracle of the new birth instantly and automatically remove this generational iniquity inheritance?

The answer from Scripture, backed up by our own experience in life seems to be – yes, no and yes – because the New Testament speaks of our salvation in three tenses – we have been saved, we are being saved and we shall be saved.

This dynamic of past, present and future is borne out in the following scriptures:

Past

The instant we come to Jesus, we are fully saved. Positionally, we have already *'received the Spirit of sonship. And by him we cry, "Abba, Father."'* (Romans 8:15, emphasis added)

> *'For it is by grace you **have been saved**, through faith – and this not from yourselves, it is the gift of God.'* (Ephesians 2:8, emphasis added)

The finished work of Christ on Calvary's cross has done everything that is needed for our salvation. We have been saved by Christ – completely, thoroughly, totally!

Present

We are being saved! Yet in experience we *'groan inwardly as **we wait** eagerly for our adoption as sons'* (Romans 8:23, emphasis added).

> *'For we are to God the aroma of Christ among those who **are being saved** and those who are perishing.'*
> (2 Corinthians 2:15, emphasis added)

> *'. . . continue to **work out** your salvation with fear and trembling.'*
> (Philippians 2:12, emphasis added)

Future

We will be saved! The adoption is certain since God has *'predestined us to be adopted as his sons'* (Ephesians 1:5).

> *'All men will hate you because of me, but he who stands firm to the end **will be saved**.'* (Mark 13:13, emphasis added)

The difference between our salvation 'positionally' and the 'out-working' of that salvation is illustrated very clearly by Paul. In 2 Corinthians 5:17, he declares,

> 'Therefore, if anyone is in Christ, he **is a new creation**; *the old has gone,* **the new has come.**'   (emphasis added)

Yet, twenty-three verses later he writes,

> '*Since we have these promises, dear friends,* **let us purify** *our-selves from everything that contaminates body and spirit,* **perfecting** *holiness out of reverence for God.*'
>
> (2 Corinthians 7:1, emphasis added)

This is not an issue of salvation. This is one of our ongoing sanctification.

Some people have actually interpreted '*he is a new creation; the old has gone, the new has come*', to mean, that on conversion everything that ever happened in our lives up to that moment has been dealt with on the cross, that there is nothing of the past that we have to visit again or deal with. If that were a true and faithful interpretation then Paul would not have had to write about so many restoration issues in his epistles to the Christians. Or as David Watson once said, 'If your theology does not equate with real life, then either your theology is defective or your real life experiences are deceptive.'

Using an Old Testament picture to illustrate this, one could say that from the moment God gave the land of Canaan to the children of Israel, it was theirs in God's eyes. Yet the reality was that the enemy who had always occupied that land had to be confronted and removed before that 'promised land' became theirs in experience.

This can be further illustrated from Paul's letter to the Colossians 3:3– 10. Our position in Christ is highlighted in bold italic type, while our present experience is in roman (normal) type:

'For you died, and your life is hidden with Christ in God. When Christ who is our life appears, then you also will appear with Him in glory. Therefore put to death your members which are on the earth: fornication, uncleanness, passion, evil desire, and covetousness, which is idolatry. *Because of these things the wrath of God is coming upon the sons of disobedience, in which you yourselves once walked when you lived in them.* But now you yourselves are to put off all these: anger, wrath, malice, blasphemy, filthy language out of your mouth. Do not lie to one another, since you have put off the old man with his deeds, *and have put on the new man who is renewed in knowledge according to the image of Him who created him.'* (NKJV)

Ken Symington relates one of many incidents of personal ministry into generational issues:

'We were out for dinner one evening with a lovely Christian couple, arguably one of the Godliest couples I have ever encountered. They "radiate" the joy of the Lord. Each of their children is truly a testimony to Godly parenting ... Over dinner the wife told us that for many years she was a manic-depressive ... So manic that many times she tried to persuade her husband to join her and the children in a mass suicide within the home. She said that to her it did not feel like depression, it just seemed "so logical".

One weekend a visiting healing/deliverance ministry came to their church and the Pastor persuaded her to have a private meeting with two of the team. That meeting changed her life. They asked her about her parents, especially her father. When she said that her father had been a member of the "Buffaloes"[2] for many years, they took her through a ministry prayer dealing with generational issues. From that moment on she was free of her manic depression.'

We have seen from Scripture how David's future generations reaped what he had sown. And we saw how their harvest of generational iniquity matched the initial seed. Therefore, we do not necessarily need to know the when and who of our ancestors' iniquity, but rather what the issue is. In other words, if there is clear evidence of a generational issue at work, then we can presume that the generational issue will be the evidence of the initial offence – and that offence needs to be brought before God.

So, when we find ourselves struggling with the same sin(s) as our previous generations, then the biblical model is *'we and our fathers have sinned against you'* in the area … of adultery/lust/ anger/violence/stealing/occult/lying, etc., … *'and they stood and confessed their sins and the iniquities of their fathers'* (Nehemiah 9:2 NKJV).

This generational issue is not meant to be complicated or 'mystical'. The reality is – what is here now is simply a result of what was sown earlier. The harvest matches the seeds and the seed matches the harvest. The 'when' and the 'who' is not as necessary to know as what the actual issue is. Having ascertained that, we then need to forgive the previous generations for leaving us such an inheritance, and lay claim to the divine exchange of the New Covenant.

Once the generational issue has been dealt with before God, Satan has lost his foothold; the demonic has lost all legal rights in our lives regarding the related issue. What a wonderful thought, to see thousands of Unionists and Nationalists being set free from the actions of their forefathers in 1912 and 1916!

A suggested approach to ministry

1. First of all, they/we must honour our father and mother (that our days may be long in the land where we live).
2. Agree with God that they/we and our forefathers have sinned against Him, naming the area being dealt with. For example, the Ulster Covenant, rebellion, lust, freemasonry.
3. Having confessed the generational issues they/we are dealing with, the finished work of Christ on the cross can then be

appropriated. The divine exchange that took place there is declared:

(a) Jesus bore our iniquity and they/we have received His pardon;

(b) He became a curse instead of us at Calvary;

(c) In Jesus' name they/we can then break off any curse that would be legally tied to them/us, due to the generational issue;

(d) Our inheritance of liberty can then be proclaimed.

4. Any ungodly ties that link you to the issue being dealt with now need to be cut. For example, if there has been occult in the generational line, cut ungodly ties to family members or friends involved in the occult.

5. In Jesus' name bind the powers of darkness that may have come down the generational line on their 'legal rights', and command them to leave. Name the likely powers: the Ulster Covenant, lust, anger, etc. Listen to the Spirit of God. It is not by might of knowledge or power of formula: it is always *'by My Spirit'*.

6. Ask the Holy Spirit to occupy areas that have now been loosed and cleansed in Jesus' Name.

7. Give thanks for the Lord's restoring grace!

A sample prayer might be...

'Heavenly Father, I thank You that I am Your child, a blood bought member of Your family. I thank You that my name is written in the Lamb's book of Life.

I am also a member of my human family and I thank You for the ancestral line that You chose to bring me into this world through. I thank You for the many and varied blessings that have flowed down this generational line to me. I especially honour my father and mother . . . .

But while I honour them, Lord, I do not agree with them in the areas where they have sinned against You. I stand with full agreement with You, Lord, in loving what is good and hating what is evil.

I identify with my forefathers and I confess that we have sinned against You. We have done this by our willing involvement in . . . .

I now unreservedly forgive my ancestors for all the things they have done which have affected and influenced me.

I also ask Your forgiveness for where I have repeated the sinful behaviour of my forefathers. As a child of God, I claim that the power of the blood of Jesus has set me free from the consequences and influences of these activities, and from all curses and pronouncements that have had an effect on my life, and from any hereditary diseases which took root in the generational line, as a result of these activities.

Jesus not only became a curse for me at Calvary and bore all my iniquities, but He also bore the consequences of those curses and iniquities, and through the divine exchange, I gratefully receive His freedom.

I declare that Satan has no rights in my life in any of these areas. They have been dealt with through the finished work of Jesus Christ at Calvary.

I now break any curse attached to these areas and ask You, Holy Spirit, to bring the life of Jesus into these areas.

Father God, I pray this in Jesus' Name.'

Notes

1. **Orange Order/Orangemen**. In his book *The Narrow Ground* A.T.Q. Stewart says: 'Because the Orange Institution has often been held to be the cause of fermenting sectarian strife it has long ago been forgotten that its birth was not the cause but the consequence of prolonged and severe sectarian conflict lasting over 20 years in a part of County Armagh. The Loyal Orange Institution was founded after the Battle of the Diamond on September 21st 1795. When the skirmish ended, the Protestants formed a circle, joined hands and declared their brotherhood in Loyalty to the Crown, the Country and the Reformed Religion.' (*Source*: http://www.grandorange.org.uk/parades/making_order.html)

Captain John Gifford, of the Royal Dublin Militia, stationed at Portadown, was present in Sloan's Inn at Loughgall when it was founded, and it is claimed that he made up the Oath and drew up the rules. As more of the gentry joined, the Institution grew so rapidly that District and County Lodges were formed. It was soon recognised that there should be some uniformity of practice and on 12th July 1796 at Portadown the idea of a Grand Lodge was mooted. (*Source*: http://www.grandorange.org.uk/history/Early_Years.html)

And so the Orange Order was birthed. A look at its website, mentioned above, is worthwhile. Despite its official frontage, many of its members are not Christians (but rather Protestant, which is more of a cultural rather than a religious identity in Northern Ireland). Many people with paramilitary associations are also associated with it.

The Orange Order has no ritual inductions, but two of its branches, the Royal Arch Purple and the Royal Black Preceptory, do have them, which historically link back into Freemasonry. *Orangeism*, Vol. 2 p. 609 states: 'The Royal Arch Purple degree, in most of its features, is not unknown to members of the Black Preceptory and the Masonic Order.'

Not only were the founding men Freemasons, but they also used the Masonic Hall as their meeting place to decide on signs, symbols, passwords, etc. It is therefore no surprise that the vast majority of Orange symbols are Masonic – the 'all seeing eye', compass, etc. It also has a Grand Master and Lodges.

The Formation of the Orange Order, p. 50 says: 'Wilson was the spokesman, and having heard his reply he invited them into the Masonic room, and then and there, satisfactory arrangements were made. As might be expected, there was nothing either refined or attractive in the words and tokens and ceremonial; but the influence of the place and its associations can be discerned in the results.'

2. **Buffaloes**. The Buffalo Lodge was founded in 1822 by William Leslie. According to their website, it is a Charitable Organisation . . . which is active at local community and national levels. The website says that they are non-political, and do not look to religion to inspire participation, describing themselves as an extended family, a social organisation, a mutually supportive group of like-minded people. Like Orangemen and Freemasons, they are organised similarly and meet in 'Lodges'. They also say, 'We are not a secret organisation, our rules and ceremonies are in the public domain.' (*Source*: Website: http://www.raobgle.org.uk)

Yet *The Origin and Development of the Royal Antediluvian Order of Buffaloes* issued by the RAOB Grand Lodge of England, p. 14, says: 'The rites and ceremonies of this lodge are based on the "old rituals" of the Order of the

Bull Mystics', and also that the Buffalo Lodge finds 'its origins in the remote past in the Bull-Worship philosophy of ancient India, Egypt, Persia, Babylon, Crete and America'.

They have a ritualistic induction procedure, and like the Orange Order they would regard themselves as a brotherhood. This gives them a strong sense of belonging, connectedness and fidelity, making it an organisation that is binding in nature.

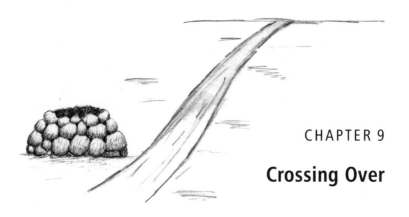

CHAPTER 9

Crossing Over

In concluding I am aware that this book is, in a sense, not finished. This may be the last chapter, but only history will tell how the journey ends. I have shared with you some of the key 'stop-overs' on my journey so far, places where I have erected my memorial stones, built an altar or stopped over for refreshing at an oasis – places of meeting with God.

Yet I believe God has given us a wonderful window of opportunity to actually write history. Having read this book, you need, I believe, to come before God and ask Him – 'Is this of You?' 'Did You give Harry those two images of "The Beaver Dam" and "The magnets" or not?' If you believe, as I do, that God has indeed spoken, then we are being called to walk the road ahead together. Where does it go? To the ultimate repenting of the Covenant by the three churches? Spiritual awakening? Revival? God alone holds the map, but that would be the desire of my heart and that of a growing body of people in this land.

If there are spiritually negative issues in our history that continue to have an effect on the present then God is calling us to be prime movers in the reconciliatory process – today! He has placed the ball in our court!

It is a ball that the Presbyterian Church in Ireland appeared to be grasping in its General Assembly in 1994 when it produced a document *The Church's Peace Vocation* (full text below). The Assembly reaffirmed it in June 2005, when it was felt that there was a necessity to nurture a deeper commitment to peace making throughout our land. If there is any purpose in this 'Peace Vocation' then surely there's a need to address this foundational issue of the Ulster Covenant!

Peace Vocation

'We, the members of the Presbyterian Church in Ireland, called by God, in the grace of Jesus Christ, and the power of the Holy Spirit, to live in faith, hope and love, as children of our heavenly Father, and witnesses to God's Kingdom, publicly acknowledge our vocation to peace, which is both the gift and mission placed on us by God.

We believe that the same evangelical faith in Jesus Christ, which emboldens us to pray to God as our heavenly Father, challenges us to develop radically new attitudes and relationships with our neighbours in Ireland.

We affirm that to be Christian peacemakers in our own situation: We must grasp more clearly the distinctive teaching of our Lord which challenges the general practice of our world, and breaks the vicious cycle of matching injury with injury, hate with hate, ignorance with ignorance. We must therefore be prepared to meet and talk together: with those in our own church with whom we have disagreements; with those from churches whose practices and beliefs differ from our own; with those from whom we are politically divided.

We affirm that to be Christian peacemakers in our own situation: we must recognise the responsibility given by God to government, and to those who serve the cause of law and order, so as to encourage well-doing, correct evil-doers, and protect the innocent. We must therefore reject violence; seek ways to advance justice and promote the welfare of the needy; affirm that in democratic societies all citizens are called to share in these responsibilities; and encourage all efforts to establish new structures of consent and participation.

We affirm that to be Christian peacemakers in our own situation: We must be initiators of programmes of action which will contribute to peace in our community. We must therefore provide resources and encouragement to enable congregations to move forward at the local level in the field of inter-community relations.

We understand peacemaking to be an affirmation and accommodation of diversity, and that our particular history in this land of divided communities and recurring violence, of mutual suspicion, fear and injury, makes it imperative that we reassert the Church's own proper calling to seek peace, and the things that make for peace in our day.'[1]

Jesus speaks about this level of integrity for all of us as Christians in the Sermon on the Mount:

> '*If you are offering your gift at the altar and there remember that **your brother has something against you**, leave your gift there in front of the altar. First **go and be reconciled** to your brother; then come and bring your gift.*' (Matthew 5:23–24, emphasis added)

God has called us:

- to love our enemies (Luke 6:27–36).
- to reach out across our social barriers as He did in His encounter with Zacchaeus (Luke 19:1–10).
- to deal with our sectarian attitudes.

This last point is made abundantly clear in His parable of the Good Samaritan, when He crossed the cultural divides of His day to minister to the Samaritan woman at the well (John 4), and also in His encounter with the Roman centurion (Matthew 8:5–13). And

His discourse from the Book of Isaiah (chapter 61) at the synagogue in Nazareth on preaching *'good news to the poor'*; proclaiming *'freedom for the prisoners'* and releasing *'the oppressed'* (see Luke 4:14– 30) certainly ruffled a few feathers!

All of these are central to His ministry of reconciling people with the Father, a ministry which He has entrusted to us and which Paul wrote about to the church in Corinth:

> *'From now on we regard **no-one** from a worldly point of view. Though we once regarded Christ in this way, we do so no longer. Therefore, **if anyone is in Christ, he is a new creation**; the old has gone, the new has come! All this is from God, who reconciled us to himself through Christ and **gave us the ministry of reconciliation**: that God was reconciling the world to himself in Christ, not counting men's sins against them. And he has **committed to us the message of reconciliation**. **We are therefore** Christ's ambassadors, as though God were making his appeal through us.'*
>
> (2 Corinthians 5:16–20, emphasis added)

What a challenging passage!

It was the challenge that God brought to many others and me in the early 1970s when we experienced a deep renewing work of the Holy Spirit. From our Protestant perspective it was all right if God was doing that to us but He was breaking the rules when He was pouring out His Spirit on Catholics as well. They, too, were clearly manifesting a deep work of the Holy Spirit in their lives, so we could no longer regard them *'from a worldly point of view'*. If they were *'in Christ'* then they were also like us – *'a new creation'*. Again from our Protestant perspective they may not have had all their theological 'i's' dotted and 't's' crossed – but then, not even all Protestant groupings can do that with each other – yet if they knew Christ as their Saviour, then we were brothers and sisters in God's family. This required a huge paradigm shift for many of us. One thing is certain – there is no second-degree citizenship in the Kingdom of God.

It was in the midst of this that the ministry of the Christian Renewal Centre was born. The Rev. Cecil Kerr, along with his wife Myrtle, took the brave step in obedience to God to purchase the Centre with the desire to see Catholics and Protestants, who had been renewed by the Holy Spirit, living out a lifestyle of reconciliation 24–7. As it turned out many other issues of reconciliation became apparent – of age, gender, personality types, cultures and theological perspectives. This was a call to live life as the 'body of Christ' *par excellence.*

To live like this constantly requires God's grace to be able to release hurt, pain, anger and grief to Him and reach out in forgiveness and be reconciled to each other. At the height of the 'troubles', as the conflict in Northern Ireland was to become known, there have been some incredible examples of people in both communities who have sought to embrace this process. The fruit of this was often seen in the development of reconciliation ministries. Here are two of them:

Gordon Wilson

'Just before 11.00am on December 8th 1987 a Provisional IRA bomb exploded without warning as people gathered at the war memorial in Enniskillen for the annual Remembrance Day service. Eleven people were killed and sixty-three injured, nine of them seriously, when the three-story gable wall of St. Michael's Reading Rooms crashed down burying people in several feet of rubble . . .

The Remembrance Day massacre shocked the world and further weakened the credibility of the Provisional IRA. Amateur video footage of the immediate aftermath of the bombing horrified people in both nationalist and unionist communities. All sides condemned the bombing. Loyalist paramilitaries were intent on retaliation but may have been stopped by the words of Gordon Wilson when he was interviewed on BBC Northern Ireland about the death of his daughter Marie.

In a voice charged with emotion Gordon Wilson's words touched the hearts of many who heard them at home and abroad. "I have lost my daughter and we shall miss her," Gordon Wilson said, "but I bear no ill will. I bear no grudge. Dirty sort of talk is not going to bring her back to life. She was a great wee lassie." ...

A group called Enniskillen Together was set up to further the cause of reconciliation in the area.'[2]

Michael McGoldrick

His son Michael was murdered by terrorists in July 1996.

'We turned on our TV and heard that a taxi driver had been murdered. I didn't think it could be anyone who belonged to us or we would have heard. But the news report continued, "Taxi driver, married with one child, wife expecting another baby ..." My wife Bridie, and I just looked at each other in cold denial. The next sentence came, "He just graduated from university on Friday." It was our son ...

The next day Bridie and I made the decision to take our own lives, because Michael was everything we had ... But as I went out to the kitchen, suddenly a picture of the crucified Christ came into my mind. It hit me that God's Son too had been murdered – for us. I knew what we had planned to do was wrong. It still amazes me how God intervened in such a miraculous way to change our minds.

Before they closed my son's coffin, I laid my hands on his and said, "Goodbye, son, I'll see you in heaven." At that very moment I experienced the power of God coursing through my body. I was filled with a great sense of joy and confidence in God. I felt as if I could have faced Goliath – I never felt as strong in my life.

On the morning of the funeral, I wrote on the back of an envelope a word which came to me so calm and clear, referring to those who had murdered Michael: "Bury your pride with your son." At the bottom I wrote, "Forgive them." I felt that, despite the agony we were going through, God had given me a message of peace, forgiveness and reconciliation. I spoke that message in front of the TV cameras that morning, and I still stand by it . . .

Since Michael's death, I have been a changed man. Along with Bridie I started a relief ministry to orphanages in Romania. I feel as if Christ has taken hold of my life and I now want to take hold of Christ and give my life to love God and serving people.'[3]

Wandering around or crossing over?

There is a deep yearning in my heart that we do not miss the way like Moses and the Children of Israel did. They had the presence of God in the pillar of fire and the cloud and yet still missed it! As a result a generation was wasted in the wilderness. I do not want to see another generation in Ireland wandering around in circles in the wilderness of our history. I want to see the next generation crossing over into God's inheritance for this land, what is becoming known as a Joshua generation or Generation X!

I do not know what lies ahead for the Ireland of tomorrow. What will the spiritual landscape look like? What I do know is that by blocking the flow of the 'river of God' in 1912, we have to a very large extent grieved and quenched the Holy Spirit in this land. In God's graciousness we experienced a move of the Holy Spirit in the 70s and 80s. One of the outcomes of that has been the development of a body of people, thousands in number, who have renounced their sectarian history.

We are also currently seeing a growing body of people who are dissatisfied with what the historic Churches in this land are serving them. They have voted with their feet. Some have gone after the other gods of the land such as materialism and humanism. Others have sought and found meaningful relationships and fellowship in newer expressions of Christian worship and in some of the historic churches that have embraced the challenge of making themselves

relevant agents of God's healing across the church and generational divides. But the legacy remains; the iniquities of our fathers
are still spiritually active. These need to be de-activated through
repentance.

As I mentioned above, I want to see the next generation
crossing over into God's inheritance for this land. Yet, the sad
and frightening reality is that many have already lost their way. As
the Irish Ombudsman Emily O'Reilly said, when speaking at a
Conference in December 2004, 'You do get a sense (in speaking to
parents with older children) of a kind of aimlessness among kids
... There is almost so much, that they cannot decide on what to
do, a lack of focus in their lives ... There are extremes in our
society (binge-drinking, suicide) that are quite frightening and go
beyond similar experiences in other western European societies.'

You only have to read the national newspapers (North and
South), even over the past few years to see this. Below are some
excerpts. Read them with your spiritual ears open. These are not
just statistics; they are about pained young people and adults made
in the image of God. They represent some of the dynamics that
are shaping our future society! I am not saying that the Ulster
Covenant is the only factor, but I believe that through the
quenching of the Holy Spirit in this way, it is a significant one.

- 'Many young men are finding it difficult to cope with life's
  problems, according to a new Irish study on male suicide.
  The study found that almost two-thirds of young men
  believe their lot is getting worse. One in three said they had
  little control over their lives. The same number rated their
  problems as "insurmountable" and felt they were being
  "pushed around in life".'   (*Irish Independent*, 09/01/04)

- 'Irish people use highly-addictive anti-depression drugs more
  than anyone else in Europe, according to evidence presented
  to the EU in Brussels yesterday ... Prescription drugs like
  Valium and Diazepam kill more people in Dublin each year

than heroin and crack cocaine while the tablets are suspected of being a major factor in suicides across the country.'

(*Irish Examiner*, 06/02/04)

- 'Young Irish men spend four times more on alcohol than any of their European neighbours, according to a major health survey released in Brussels yesterday.'

(*Irish Independent*, 9/3/04)

- 'While cannabis is the most widely used illegal substance among Irish people, cocaine is rapidly growing in popularity. Some 4.8% of young adults, aged between 15 and 34, have used the drug at some point in their lives, more than in any other State in the EU – apart from the UK and Spain.'

(*Irish Times*, Health Supplement, 20/04/04)

- 'Eight in every ten Irish adults were under the legal age when they first had sex, according to new research ... A survey paints a picture of a country with low moral standards both before and after marriage ... The study also showed that only one in ten believe you should remain a virgin until after marriage.'   (*Irish Independent*, 08/07/04)

- 'Three out of five reported cases of child sex abuse are perpetrated by a male relative, while a further quarter are carried out by a person known to the victim, apart from a direct family member, the Dublin Rape Crisis Centre (DRCC) said yesterday ... One in five callers to the DRCC's 24-hour helpline last year was aged 15–17 ... A total of 11,863 counselling calls were received.'

(*Irish Examiner*, 20/07/04)

- 'Three out of every twenty marriages end in divorce, with a record number of terminations granted by the courts last year ... According to the annual report of the Courts Service, 2,929 couples were granted a divorce last year.'

(*Irish Examiner*, 16/07/04)

- 'Six times as many children are born outside marriage than in 1980 ... The latest EU population figures reveal one-in-three Irish births was outside marriage. Our rate of 31% is 1% higher than the EU average. The comparative figure in 1980 was 5%.' *(Irish Examiner,* 02/09/04)

  'Sociologists say that the two main factors are – changing social norms and changing attitudes towards the church.'
  (Irish Times, 17.07.05)

- 'Hundreds of Ulster children, some as young as 13, are being lured into prostitution across the province ... And family members are involved in grooming children for paedophile rings, the investigation (by BBC Northern Ireland) will say.'
  (Belfast Telegraph, 20/09/04)

- 'Latest research has found that young Irish people are gambling with unprotected intercourse and getting caught ... According to the CPA (Crisis Pregnancy Agency), 30% of Irish teens are now sexually active. "In one of our Dublin clinics the average age of sexual activity is 16," says Niall Behan, chief executive of the Irish Family Planning Association. "We even see children as young as 12 who are sexually active."' *(Irish Independent,* 28/09/04)

- 'Women's Aid, which runs a national help line for women suffering from physical, sexual and emotional abuse mostly from husbands or partners, have reported that in 2003 they had 18,902 phone calls. "Reports ranged from outright rape in front of their children to scalding and burns, beatings and strangulations..."' *(Irish Times,* 13.01.05)

- 'Former Social Democratic Labour Party MP John Hume has recently launched a fundraising drive for a prevention service to address the "devastating problem" of suicide. The latest figures (for the end of 2003) show that 444 people died by suicide (80% were male) and that there were 11,200 attempted suicides. The biggest barriers to prevention were people's inability to talk about their distress, to communicate their pain and ask for help.' *(Irish Times,* 12.04.05)

- 'Dr. Sean Brady, Catholic Primate for Ireland, speaking at a recent ecumenical service in Cork said that "living one's faith in Jesus has become increasingly difficult in a social and cultural setting in which that faith is constantly challenged." He went on to say, "It is sometimes easier to be identified as an agnostic than as a believer ... unbelief, or hostility to faith is self-explanatory, whereas belief needs a sort of legitimisation."' *(Irish Times,* 06.05.05)

- 'Doctors in Northern Ireland are struggling to cope with an explosion in Sexually Transmitted Diseases – 1,321 teenagers, two thirds of them girls, contacted sex health clinics this year, after catching serious diseases such as syphilis (22 girls and 1 boy were under the age of 14). Five children have HIV and 4 under the age of 14 have the virus.'

  (Belfast Telegraph, 02.11.05)

- 'Regarding anti-social behaviour among young people, one Independent TD in Dublin in a recent Government debate stressed, "This is not just a policing issue but a parents' issue. Where there are strong, healthy, vibrant, stable families, there is less anti-social behaviour."'

  (Irish Times, 11.11.05)

One encouraging sign is the growing number of young people who are finding God in a new and radical way having tried many of the things society has had to offer. Many of them are not interested in denominations or maintaining old buildings. What they are interested in is intimacy with God. In that place they are experiencing healing, finding out who they are. This is then being worked out in compassionate ministry to the needy and marginalised and by a desire to see God transforming our society.

At a recent gathering of young people who are embracing the growing 24–7 prayer movement,[4] I was deeply touched to see at the entrance of the prayer room a cross with the British and Irish flags laid at its foot. These are young people with a 'Kingdom of God' vision, whose hearts' desire is, 'God, may Your Kingdom come, may Your will be done in Ireland, as it is in heaven.' They realise that Ireland may have been partitioned in 1922, but spiritually it is still a single entity. Is it not strange that the majority of Churches in this land also believe it? As I have already mentioned in a previous chapter the Catholic, Church of Ireland, Methodist, Presbyterian, Baptist churches are all thirty-two county churches.

Whatever happens politically regarding the border, I believe God is calling us to lay down our idolatry over the land. To be able to say as a Christian from a Unionist background, 'God, if You can further Your Kingdom purposes for Ireland, through a united Ireland, that is alright with me', or as a Christian from a Nationalist background, you can embrace the reverse scenario, would truly enable us to place the future in God's hands and to disempower Satan's grip on the idol we have made out of our national identities.

One thing is sure, whatever the political landscape of tomorrow will look like; a new spiritual wineskin is emerging. Are we big enough to encourage it, to mentor it, to be fathers and mothers to it and this Joshua generation? What if a vast majority of our historic denominational churches close in the next five to ten years? It does not take a prophet to tell us that this is already happening and will increasingly do so, especially in the rural areas. Is that alright with us, or have they also become idols to us? A growing number of our churches have a 'sell by' date on them. Some of them are locked into our history, into church politics and internal power struggles, into Orange-ism and Freemasonry. They are incapable of embracing change and especially the changing Christian culture of our young people. They are signing their own Death Certificate.

Unlike Moses of old and his generation, we do not have to die in the wilderness; we can cross over with this Joshua generation. They will need us, and when you talk to them, they will tell you that they want us to be mothers and fathers in the faith to them. Many young people who have found Christ in recent years have never known loving fathers in the natural. As God heals them from the resulting deficits they will need us to model fatherhood, parenthood to them, both naturally and spiritually.

Some practical steps

There will undoubtedly be people who on reading this book will immediately dismiss it. Some may do so because they are under the control of the spiritual stronghold of the Covenant, which I mentioned in Chapter 6. If, however, as you have read this book there is a resonance of agreement in your spirit about it, then there are a number of options/possibilities open to you at a personal and a corporate level. Please do not set this 'agreement in your spirit' aside but rather pray about it, asking God what response He would have you to make. Some of these I will mention below, you may think of others:

- Cut off the power of the Covenant over your own life and family as mentioned in the previous chapter, if you have not already done so.
- Pray for a move of God's Spirit throughout Ireland to bring us as Christians to a place of humbling ourselves before Him in repentance for the divisions in the Church and the sectarian attitudes that we have held unto. We need to see the Church in Ireland make a fresh covenant with Him, giving Him back the Church and Ireland (North and South) so that His will may be done, His kingdom may come here, as it is in heaven. The urgency of this is all the more significant when one realises that in 2012 we will be having the one hundredth anniversary of the Ulster Covenant, when

there will undoubtedly be a lot of pressure placed on the
Protestant Churches in Ireland to play a leading role in those
celebrations and commemorations.

- Get as many of your friends as possible to read this book. Along
  with some of them who agree with the findings here, form a
  prayer group to intercede in humility for the clergy – especially
  of the Churches involved in endorsing the Ulster Covenant in
  1912. This is a spiritual battle! As part of the spiritual leadership
  in Ireland today they ultimately need to lead us in repentance
  of the Ulster Covenant at a church governmental level. (More
  copies of this book are available from the Christian Renewal
  Centre or from your local Christian Bookshop.) Similarly,
  we also need to pray for our politicians.

- Talk with your own spiritual and political leaders about the
  contents of this book and about what you would like to see
  happen.

- If you are a member of the Irish clergy reading this book –
  especially from the Presbyterian, Church of Ireland or
  Methodist Churches – I would ideally love to see something
  of a 'working party' established in each of them in preparation for a resolution regarding repentance coming into the
  respective governing bodies. Can you be an initiator of or
  participant in such a group? God is looking for people in these
  Churches with the same spirit as Jonathan and his armour-
  bearer in 1 Samuel 14, when he rose up and took the initiative
  in attacking the Philistines:

> ' "Come, **let's go over** . . . perhaps the LORD will act on our behalf.
> Nothing can hinder the LORD from saving, whether by many or by
> few." "Do all that you have in mind," his armour-bearer said,
> "Go ahead; I am with you heart and soul." '
>
> (1 Samuel 14:6–7, emphasis added)

In using this scripture I am not in any way advocating violent
action, but rather applying the spiritual principle contained in
it of rising up in faith and taking the initiative!

- I am also aware that other Irish Churches played their part in supporting resistance to Home Rule i.e. the Congregational, Reformed Presbyterian and Baptist Churches. They too need to look at the issue of repentance regarding the part they played. If you are a leader or member of one of those denominations ask God 'Is there anything You would have me to do about it?'
- I am open to discuss this further with individuals or denominational groups if this increases understanding and ownership of the issues I have shared with you in this book. Obviously there are limitations regarding distance, diaries, etc., but nevertheless do contact me.
- I am also conscious that God is putting the issue of the Ulster Covenant on people's hearts not only here in Ireland but in other places around the world. There are a growing number of Christians among the Irish Diaspora in places like the USA and Australia who have a burden to pray for Ireland. If you know of anyone in this category or in other Prayer Networks that pray for Ireland, do let them know about this book so that they can also stand with us in intercession regarding this issue of the Covenants – both the Ulster Covenant and the Sinn Fein Covenant.

I leave you with some words of incredible hope, by returning to the original image of the beaver's dam which I shared with you at the beginning of this book. In that image I continue to see so clearly all that water held back by it – the river of God, the Holy Spirit. This I believe is why God showed me it in the first place; He wants to pour out His Spirit on our land; He wants to bring healing to us. That is His declaration of intent. To make moves in the direction of seeing the log of the Ulster Covenant removed from the dam is therefore an act of faith and hope for the future of Ireland. ' . . . *where the river flows everything will live*' (Ezekiel 47:9).

And also with Moses' last words . . .

> *'See, I set before you today life and prosperity, death and destruction. For I command you today to love the* LORD *your God, to walk in his ways, and to keep his commands, decrees and laws; then you will live and increase, and the* LORD *your God will bless you in the land you are entering to possess.*
>
> *But if your heart turns away and you are not obedient, and if you are drawn away to bow down to other gods and worship them, I declare to you this day that you will certainly be destroyed. You will not live long in the land you are crossing the Jordan to enter and possess.*
>
> *This day I call heaven and earth as witnesses against you that I have set before you life and death, blessings and curses. Now choose life, so that you and your children may live and that you may love the* LORD *your God, listen to his voice, and hold fast to him. For the* LORD *is your life, and he will give you many years in the land he swore to give to your fathers, Abraham, Isaac and Jacob.'*   (Deuteronomy 30:15–20)

. . . and also space for your own use as you respond. This is not just a gimmicky way of finishing a book. The space is provided, because I sense that God is asking you to prayerfully seek His face and determine in faith to answer this question – 'How would you like to see this chapter finish?'

Write on . . .

- *My prayer is that . . .*

Write on . . .

- *I would like to see . . .*

Write on . . .

- *My commitment is to . . .*

Notes

1. *Source*: The Press Office of The Presbyterian Church in Ireland website – www.presbyterianireland.org
2. *Source*: www.bbc.co.uk/history/war/troubles/agreement/ennibomb.shtml
3. *Source*: www.powertochange.ie/changed/michael_mcgoldrick.html
4. A must read is *Red Moon Rising* by Pete Greg, published by Kingsway Publications.

Further Letters to the *Belfast Newsletter* in 1912, as Mentioned in Chapter 1

12/7/12: Part of an Editorial

The Chairman, who met with a very hearty reception, said they were gathered together again to celebrate, as in years gone by, the memorable victory of the Boyne – that victory which, for 222 years, at any rate had put an end to the rule of the Church of Rome in the British Empire, and delivered this country from tyranny and arbitrary power. Ever since the day when James retired, defeated from the banks of the Boyne before the triumphant troops of William, Rome had been endeavouring in every manner to retrieve the supremacy in this country which she lost that day. Schemes and plots of every description had been employed by her adherents to achieve that object, but on every occasion they had failed. To live on terms of equality was no use to them. Supremacy was what they sought, and supremacy was what they, on that glorious anniversary, solemnly decided they never should have ... It was the Protestant religion which had made the British Empire. The open Bible had been the secret of England's greatness. Protestantism stood for the liberties and rights of all men and each, under the Union Jack, was enabled to worship God according to his own conscience without the interference of any man.

Things and manners had changed very much since those days, but the object of the Church of Rome never changed. It was not now a question of deposing the Protestant Monarch, but the object was the deposing of the Protestant religion and establishing the Roman Catholic religion in its stead. Rome was not only a symbol of religion – she was a political institution as well, and that fact brought them to the present day. For many years the Church of Rome had been gradually losing the supremacy, which at one time she had over the Christian world ... In Ireland alone, or rather in a part of it, her domination was as firm as ever ... Ireland was the basis of her operations, and from that basis she was endeavouring with all her might, to re-conquer England. They knew that Home Rule meant Rome Rule and, if once the former were established, the latter would follow as a matter of course. For years attacks had been made on the British Constitution in order to pave the way and prepare the ground for the final attack. In 1886 and in 1893 these attacks were repulsed. On the latter occasion the iniquitous Home Rule measure was hurled back in the teeth of those who would have broken up the British Empire by the House of Lords, and the British nation applauded and approved their action.

Another attack on the Constitution has been successfully made, and the House of Lords had had its powers curtailed, and having disposed of that great attack, the whole force was now being concentrated for the final assault. He believed history would repeat itself. Two hundred and twenty-four years ago a powerful army appeared before a city and demanded admission. Counsels were divided, and all appeared to be lost, but thirteen noble lads, whose memory should never fade – heedless of opposition, regardless of what the consequence might be – seized the keys, shut the gates in their teeth, and with shouts of 'No Surrender' altered what might have been the history of the world.

At the present moment they had another army, serving the same masters, at their very gates. What reception would that army receive? Should they, the descendants of the men who suffered famine and privations, but never would yield, now become cravens and place their neck beneath the yoke their fathers scorned – or should they keep unstained the heritage they handed down to them? Ulster was resolved. They had made their declaration. They pledged their word at Craigavon, they confirmed it at Balmoral on Easter Tuesday, and they pledged themselves again that day. They sent over the sea a message to Sir Edward Carson and Mr. Bonar Law and all those Unionist members so nobly doing battle in the House of Commons, that their hearts were as their hearts, and that they were prepared to face any dangers they might be called upon to undertake to retain their position as citizens of the British Empire under the Imperial Parliament. They would never, in Ulster, submit to be ruled by John Redmond, Joe Devlin, and a Dublin Parliament ... The men at Derry did more than shout 'No Surrender'. They shut the gates, but before they shut the gates they had made ample preparation for the siege. That was what they were doing, and what they must do, with perpetual and renewed vigour.

It was a grand sight to see their men marching to Balmoral. He had longed for the day when their men should be properly organised. They were doing well now, but they must do better. Every man must learn, at no matter what inconvenience, to take his place in the battle. Now was the time to prepare. Let them perfect their organisation in every way. Let them keep on drilling, so that when the time came they would be enabled to hurl back those would-be masters of theirs, as their fathers hurled back the forces of Popish James from the walls of Derry, and then gave them their final rout 222 years ago on the banks of the Boyne.

26/8/12: Article – 'Religious aspects of Home Rule' by Rev. R.W. Colquhoun, Vicar of Ventor, Isle of Wight

The Ulster people look upon the Home Rule proposals of the Government as a challenge, and they have not been slow in their response. Drilling is going on nightly, and rifle clubs are being formed in all leading centres. The Protestant people are not alone in this. A newspaper report to hand gives the information that some three hundred five and six chambered revolvers have been delivered to the Belfast Nationalists. It will be seen, therefore, that the country is preparing for civil war ... There are certain difficulties in the way of a correct understanding of the situation in Ireland, which ought to be removed. The first and foremost is the religious one. The political question in Ireland is simply a matter of religious belief.

English newspapers in their articles, and English politicians in their speeches, are willing to view Home Rule as a political problem. Those who live in Ireland and who know the real state of affairs are perfectly well aware that the question is not political in the sense in which that word is understood in England. The dividing line in Ireland is the religious one. The rank and file Roman Catholic is Irish, and almost to a man they are Nationalists and Home Rulers: the Protestants are Unionists ... In the North there is a handful of Protestant Home Rulers who are chiefly settlers from England and Scotland, living there for trade purposes, and prepared to sacrifice their religious convictions for the sake of their radical principles.

Rightly or wrongly, the people of Ulster to-day look upon Home Rule as Rome Rule, and are firmly persuaded that government by Messrs. Redmond and Devlin and their followers would simply mean government by the priests and leaders of the Roman Catholic Church. It is true that the supporters of the present Bill have been lavish in their promises of safeguards and guarantees under the new regime. The Protestants, however, may well ask how it will be possible for a Parliament under the control of Rome to recognise any safeguards.

The financial condition of Ireland is largely a matter of religion also. The poverty of the people in the Roman Catholic districts of the South and West is well known, but few really understand how far the Church is responsible for the state of things. Readers of Mr. Michael McCarthy's books are aware that the ecclesiastical establishments in Ireland are out of all proportion to the population of the country. The support of these vast institutions makes a demand upon the people which drains their resources to the last farthing ... the claims of the Church must be met, no matter who suffers, and it is not an unreasonable assumption that with a Roman Catholic majority in power every effort would be made by the priesthood to obtain public funds for the furtherance of the work of the Church.

6/9/12: *Letter to the Editor*

Sir – The following extract from *The Coming Dominion of Rome in Britain*, a remarkable book recently published should be read with interest in Ulster: 'There cannot be a doubt that Home Rule, or the separation of Ireland from England, emanates from Rome and the Jesuits, and that its object is to enable Rome to obtain supreme power in Ireland. The Jesuits having now complete control over the Vatican and the priesthood of Rome, that dominion will be the dominion of the Jesuits. The past history of the Jesuits shows what the Protestants of Ireland may expect when Rome has obtained supreme power in that country. For it was the Jesuits, and they alone, who have been responsible for all the massacres of Protestants and wars against them in the past. We may also be sure that they have not neglected to foster the hatred of Irish Catholics against Protestants living amongst them, although in accordance with their policy, this hatred was to be "dissembled so as not to transpire until the day when it shall be appointed to break forth".

The guarantees to be given by the British Government against injustice and religious persecution may serve to quiet the elastic consciences of Protestant Radicals, but they would be of little avail against the above mentioned hate when allowed to break forth, and would be speedily swept aside by the Jesuits once they were in power. Yet Home Rule is supported by nearly the whole of the Nonconformist Radicals. Their pastors advocate it from the pulpit, and denounce those who oppose it as traitors, although the term might be more justly applied to those who betray their brethren and co-religionists into the hands of the people who hate them. It would seem as if Radicalism destroyed Protestantism, and the true explanation of this is that the unbelief which underlies the revolutionary spirit kills the conscience and makes the extreme Radical an easy victim of Jesuit agitators.

There are also certain English Nonconformists, who had hitherto been regarded as champions of Protestantism, but who have laboured to find an excuse for supporting Home Rule, asking, forsooth, what evidence there is in the facts of history and the nature of Romanism that

Home Rule means Rome Rule. They choose to shut their eyes to the fact that the Irish supporters of Home Rule are representatives of the priesthood and the Jesuits, and members of the murderous secret societies whose one aim is the extermination of Protestants ... The result is that the Nonconformist Radicals have become the mainstay of Rome's political ambition ... The determined attempt made by Mr. Winston Churchill to force the Ulster Protestant to listen to his speech on Home Rule ... indicated a resolute determination on the part of the Government to force Home Rule on Ulster, and betrays their wholehearted support of Rome's policy. The fact that 4,000 troops were brought into Belfast to repress any rising, seems to foreshadow an intention on the part of the Government to force Home Rule on Ulster by making use of armed forces of the Crown to put down any resistance to the legislative acts of Catholic Rulers. One may be mistaken, but it is exactly what Jesuits would do when they are in power.'

Yours truly,
Presbyterian.

20/9/12: Colonel Leslie and the Covenant – Glaslough Unionist Club

A special meeting of the Glaslough Unionist Club was held in the hall, Glaslough, on the night of the 16th inst. to consider, amongst other things, the establishment of a miniature rifle club.

The Chairman said he was glad to see that since the inauguration of the club, the membership had increased from 43 to 87. He had not had an opportunity yet of witnessing the members drilling, but hoped to have the opportunity on the occasion of their next drill. Their idea was to be in readiness for any emergency that might arise, and he was glad to know the men of Glaslough were not going to be behind in this matter. They had practically decided to form a miniature rifle club such as was in connection with a great many other Unionist clubs in Ulster.

He hoped that they would all attend the great demonstration at Enniskillen and so give expression of their opinion 'with regard to Home Rule'. Later on, on Ulster Day, they would be asked to sign the Solemn Covenant. He was glad to know that in that district there was going to be a great united service in Glenarm Presbyterian Church prior to the signing of the Covenant.

24/9/12: Part of a speech by Mr McCaw at a demonstration at Dromore

'A Roman Catholic had just as much right to the exercise of his own faith without let or hindrance as a Protestant had. That was a fact which no one there would dispute, and so long therefore, as Roman Catholics confined themselves to the exercise of their own religion the Protestants had no quarrel with them. But, as was well known to them, all politics were so much mixed up with and took such an important place in the Roman Catholic religion that it was very difficult to disentangle the one from the other (hear, hear). It was, however, the political side of the Roman Catholic religion and not in any way with the exercise of their faith that they Protestants had grounds for quarrel. Experience had taught them that when the Roman Catholic Church had the opportunity it always sought to make its own religion the ruling and dominant force.'

29/9/12: Rev. Dr Brown and the signing of the Covenant – at a meeting yesterday of the Glasgow Presbytery of the Church of Scotland – 'Scottish Presbyterians and Home Rule'

There were times in connection with foreign policy of our country when party divisions fell, when the nation realised that they must stand together as one man and with one heart and will fight for the nation's cause ... People might sneer at their movement, but we believe that the men of Ulster in signing the Covenant were as true and as earnest as their forefathers when, at the Church of Greyfriars, they signed the National Covenant (Hear, hear). Who ever read of a great nation seeking to cast out her loyal subjects? Who ever doubted that the men of Ulster were loyal sons of Britain?

The Covenant Exported

In September 2004 I was preparing to go to America to attend a one week Residential Course with the International Reconciliation Coalition, founded by John Dawson (author of *Taking Your Cities for God* and *Healing America's Wounds*). It was part of a web-based course on Reconciliation that I was doing. I had to write up assignments on various aspects of reconciliation and post them to the website. The last question I had to reflect on and respond to was, 'Is there any people group(s) that your people group needs to be reconciled with?' As I reflected on this God brought to mind two people groups – the Irish Catholic Diaspora in the United States and the other one, which rather surprised me at the time, was the First Nation people of North America.

As part of my research I picked off my shelves a book which I was given during a previous trip to the States three years earlier, entitled *Wherever the Green is Worn: the Story of the Irish Diaspora* by Tim Pat Coogan.[1] Below are come excerpts from the opening chapters:

> 'Some 70 million people on the globe are entitled to call themselves Irish – a remarkable statistic when one considers that there are only five million people on the island of Ireland itself,

and of these at least 800,000 living in North-Eastern Ireland say they are not Irish at all and describe themselves as British!

The Irish Diaspora is the outworking of two forms of colonialism, those of Mother England and Mother Church (the Catholic Church) ... So much of the Irish Diaspora's view of themselves and of their nationality is coloured by the happenings in Northern Ireland. So many ideas of Irish identity have been formed by, with, or from Britain.

Today the results of the greatest scattering of the centuries are chiefly located in North America and in the United Kingdom. From the 1920s onward, Britain became the prime destination for Irish emigrants. Perhaps eight out of ten Irish who left the country in the immediate post-Second World War years headed for the United Kingdom. In general, the pattern of Irish emigration was laid down in the sixteenth century. When invasion began in earnest under Elizabeth I, and the Anglican Reformation was superimposed on Ireland, Catholic Irish emigration may be said to have begun in a major way. In the sixteenth and seventeenth centuries there were four separate waves of emigration stemming from the wars in Ireland ... Cromwell transported several thousands from Ireland to the West Indies and to Virginia. It may be that as many as 35,000 men were shipped out, some 12,000 including women to the West Indies. Later in the seventeenth century, after the Protestant victory which resulted in the Treaty of Limerick in 1691, the celebrated flight of the "Wild Geese" took place. In this exodus, well in excess of 20,000 men set sail for the regiments of Catholic France, accompanied by their wives and children.

Then the great cataclysm of the Famine befell in the 1840s. A huge shoaling outward of panic-stricken people occurred, and Ireland suffered a physical and psychological shock from which it is probably true to say the country and its people are only recovering in our time. A million died and probably as many as two-and-a-half million people left Ireland in the decade 1845–1855.

They left their country and they founded an empire – for Mother Church ... It is calculated that from 1855 to the outbreak of the Great War in 1914, over and above the Famine departures, a further four million left Ireland. Their impact on the world was so colossal that in America for example, it is estimated that some 38 million of the 43 million who at U.S. Census time give their ethnic origin as Irish, are of Catholic origin.

It could be said that the real foundations of modern emigration to America lay in an "Act to prevent the further growth of Popery", passed by the British Parliament in the year 1704. The Act enjoined a Sacramental Test on all citizens of the realm, forcing them to take an oath of loyalty to the Established Church (Church of England). By this Act the Presbyterians were as much discriminated against as were the Catholics, but they had an edge over their Catholic counterparts inasmuch as they had a little money and, very often, a trade. This gave them an independence of action and a certain rudimentary support system which, along with a sturdy independent spirit, made them successful colonists.'

It was the last paragraph mentioned above and in particular the mention of the Presbyterian people that caught my attention; connections were being made in my mind...

The North America's First Nation People

A few months earlier an American lady called Daphne Swilling, who has a real heart for reconciliation in Ireland, had visited me. She shared her burden for the First Nation People and the Trail of Tears (which, up to that point I was ignorant of!). Part of it related to the Irish Scots (or Ulster-Scot Presbyterians) who went to America with the same stuff they brought to Ireland from Scotland during the plantation – a wrong understanding of Old Testament Covenant – appropriating to themselves God's relationship to the Jews (as a people) and to Israel (as a land). As she shared I was deeply impacted in my spirit and started to weep.

Daphne left me with a small book called *The Trail of Tears* by R. Conrad Stein (published by Children's Press, 1993). Here are a few excerpts from it:

'In 1828, two events shaped the destiny of the Cherokee nation. First, Andrew Jackson (whose parents were Presbyterian from Carrickfergus, Co. Antrim, N. Ireland) was elected as the 7th president of the United States ... Like many pioneers, Jackson carried with him a deeply ingrained hostility towards the Indians. Second, gold was discovered at Dahlonega, Georgia, which was deep in the Cherokees Territory. This development had an immediate and dramatic effect on the Cherokee people ... Many of the miners stole Indian cattle and attacked Indian women ... Gangs of rowdies rode into Cherokee country to start fires and plunder homes.

Eventually, a Cherokee lawsuit reached the United States Supreme Court ... After a series of decisions, the court ruled in 1832 that the federal government must protect the Cherokee nation from its many intruders ... In an historic defiance of the Supreme Court's authority, President Jackson overruled it. Moreover, President Jackson ... called for the removal, by force if necessary, of all Indians to east of the Mississippi River. May 1838, saw the beginning of a 400 mile forced trek westward to Oklahoma (now known as the Trail of Tears) of an estimated seventeen thousand Cherokees, during which it is estimated one in every four died.'

Since then I have found other writings confirming what God was doing within me:

1. *Honor*, written by Fawn Parish, one of the Reconciliation Course organisers (published by Renew, a division of Gospel Light)

'Some historians say that as many as eight hundred times we broke treaty after treaty with the Indians. In many cases the treaties were broken with unspeakable brutality ... in the hostile actions against tribe after tribe, in the confiscation of land, in the repeated lies of treaty upon treaty, the Great White Father's words were not honoured. When Christians came to proclaim the covenantal treaty God had made for them, it was too late.

As recently as thirty years ago, Native American children were dragged from their families and placed in "residential schools". They were forbidden to speak their own language or observe their own customs. In these schools, children were beaten and shamed for being Indian, many times in the name of Christ. No wonder Fern Noble, a Native American Christian asks, "Why do so few of my people believe in You?" The numbers are pitifully few. Less that 5 percent are Christians. Most in fact, have suffered from alcoholism. Suicide is five times higher for Native Americans than for any other ethnic group, and the average life expectancy is only 40 years.'

2. *The Making of America: How the Scots-Irish Shaped a Nation* by Billy Kennedy (published by Ambassador, Causeway Press)

'Bitter experience of religious discrimination and economic deprivation were major factors for many of them after their movement from the north of Ireland to America through the 18th century from about 1717 (*quite often from the British Crown*).'

(p. 13, emphasis added)

The Scots-Irish battles with the Indian tribes in the years leading up to, during and after the Revolutionary War were quite decisive in creating the American nation. Indeed, the major events from 1755 to 1790 centred around the Appalachian territory and the gaps in them where the frontier settlers had to enter to progress towards the new lands.'

(p. 16)

'The Wataugans (the first batch were 16 families from North Carolina, mostly Scots-Irish led by Colonel John Sevier and Colonel James Robertson) moved on to lands that were officially designated Cherokee country, much to the consternation of Lord

Dunmore, the royal governor of Virginia. An incensed Dunmore reported back to London that there were "a set of people in the back country of the colony, bordering on Cherokee country, who, finding they could not obtain the land they fancied here, have set up a separate state." ...

The Watauga Presbyterian settlers used the theology of **manifest destiny** to define their attitudes to far-off London rule, maintaining: "If God did not want us to have this land, we would not be out here." As was the case in Ulster during the 17th century Scottish Plantation there, so it was in the 18th century settlements of the Appalachian backcountry, as God intended.

This was meant to be, and, with such a mindset, the Scots-Irish found the courage, determination and feeling that they were doing God's will in settling along the American frontier and pushing civilisation to the outer limits.'   (p. 19, emphasis added)

I find the whole dynamic of 'manifest destiny' utterly repugnant and as Kennedy points out it is so akin to the dynamics behind the Plantation in Ulster. I find it incredible how we can on one hand justify these aspects of the birthing of the United States of America (as this book appears to be doing) and on the other hand strongly denounce the Apartheid Regime in South Africa (as many of us rightly did), when both along with the Plantation of Ulster had the same theological error at their roots.

What I needed to know as I went to America that month was – has anybody from Ireland done anything about this? Will there be anyone – particularly a First Nation person whose ancestors were involved with the whole Trail of Tears issue – on this course that I need to pray with? There wasn't but I did meet some First Nation people who helped me understand and identify with some of the pain they continue to feel over the past injustices of the white man.

Since then Daphne Swilling has brought to Ireland some of the ancestors of the nations dispossessed of land by Andrew Jackson. During their visit I had the privilege of being part of a reconciliation gathering with them and also of going to Nashville, Tennessee to participate in a First Nations Reconciliation Conference. There is such a deep woundedness in these dear people and thankfully God is raising up a number of them who want to see healing in Christ for their people.

Note

1. Published in 2001 by Palgrave. Reproduced with permission of Palgrave Macmillan.

The Christian Renewal Centre – a *House of Prayer for Ireland*

The Community at the Christian Renewal Centre was founded in 1974 as a group of Christians drawn together by God from different Churches, e.g. Catholic and Protestant and since then also from the new Community and Fellowship Churches.

While remaining members of these Churches, we seek, through the power of the Holy Spirit to demonstrate and proclaim the uniting love of Jesus Christ, our Saviour and Lord.

God called us to pray and work for reconciliation, through prayer and renewal, in His Church in Ireland and abroad. About five years ago we became conscious with the changes in Ireland – spiritual, political and social – that God was calling us to redefine this vision. Ireland is still our primary field of ministry, reconciliation and renewal are still central to our work, but the key area of emphasis in ministry is prayer. Prayer for a **new outpouring of the Holy Spirit** in reconciliation, renewal and revival.

A House of Prayer

Prayer

Recognising the transforming power of God through prayer, we, as a community, are committed to prayer in its many forms – worship, intercession, petition, thanksgiving, supplication, etc.

Together we seek to:

- grow in our understanding and practice of prayer and in particular intercession
- call other Christians to come together for prayer and intercession, and
- help them to pray effectively by:
  - developing and organising training programmes
  - promoting prayer strategies

And also to be a place:

- of meeting/conversing with God
- of intimacy – of sharing our hearts with Him. This includes the possibility of personal encounter/change as we seek Him
- where we listen to God as He shares His heart and mind with us, for others and Ireland

We pray for:

Reconciliation
We acknowledge our share in the shame of division in the Church, which is an offence to Christ, resulting in broken fellowship and ultimately, in sectarian violence.

We affirm that '[Christ] *is our peace, who has made the two one and has destroyed the barrier, the dividing wall of hostility'* (Ephesians 2:14).

Therefore, we encourage and facilitate the coming together of people, in an atmosphere of prayer and worship, allowing the Spirit to:

- melt our hearts
- lead us into repentance, and forgiveness of one another
- enable us to accept and honour one another in Christ, thus restoring fellowship

We acknowledge that our sins – personal/corporate, past/present – give Satan a foothold in our lives and in society (Ephesians 4:27), which hinders a change in hearts and minds. Confession and repentance remove that foothold, and enable the reconciling power of Christ to bring healing to people and situations. This often takes place in a powerful way within the context of united intercession.

We also recognise that Satan seeks to pervert the gifts God gives to nations. It is our desire that God's gifts for Ireland (e.g. mission sending, arts, hospitality, etc.) be clearly revealed, restored and offered back to Him for His glory.

Renewal

Being committed to Jesus Christ as Saviour and Lord, who baptises us in the Holy Spirit and renews His Church, we work with Him to encourage:

- personal renewal
- renewal in the local Church
- restoration of the gifts of the Holy Spirit

so that His Church may be an effective witness to His power and healing love for the world.

These may happen in the context of: conferences, monthly Days of Refreshing, Prayer Leaders' Days, special days of intercession for Ireland, Retreats, Prayer Schools etc., in the Centre. Similar activities can be arranged outside in Prayer Groups, Churches, Fellowships etc.

Revival

There has been an increased awareness in many people (here in Ireland and in various parts of the world) – through prayer, the inner witness of the Holy Spirit and through the prophetic word – that God is preparing Ireland for revival. In the history of revivals, many have been preceded by a movement of prayer. We believe God is wanting us, as a Community, to be a part of such a movement.

There are two main groups of people we pray specifically for – the Church and the young adults. We are very conscious that what happens to these two groups will determine the future direction Ireland will take – for good or for evil.

Through our united prayer, witness and shared proclamation of the Gospel, we aim by God's grace to challenge the principalities and powers of sectarianism and division, and to be a prophetic sign and visual aid to the Church and to the unbelieving world.

Further information

Please contact us at:

The Christian Renewal Centre – *a House of Prayer for Ireland*
44 Shore Road
Rostrevor
Co. Down
BT34 3ET
Northern Ireland

or go to our website:

www.crc-rostrevor.org

Further Resources

Taking Your Cities for God by John Dawson (published by Charisma House)

Intercessory Prayer by Dutch Sheets, (published by Regal a division of Gospel Light)

The River of God by Dutch Sheets (published by Renew a division of Gospel Light)

Sins of the Fathers by Brian Mills and Roger Mitchell (published by Sovereign World)

Red Moon Rising by Pete Greg (published by Kingsway Publications)

The Transformations Video and DVD series (published by Sentinel Ministries)

We hope you enjoyed reading this New Wine book.
For details of other New Wine books
and a range of 2,000 titles from other
Word and Spirit publishers visit our website:
www.newwineministries.co.uk